Post-Communist Cultural Studies Series

Thomas Cushman, General Editor

The Culture of Lies
Antipolitical Essays
Dubravka Ugrešić

Burden of Dreams
History and Identity in Post-Soviet Ukraine
Catherine Wanner

Gender Politics in the Western Balkans
Women, Society, and Politics in Yugoslavia and the
Yugoslav Successor States
Sabrina P. Ramet, ed.

The Culture of Power in Serbia
Nationalism and the Destruction of Alternatives
Eric D. Gordy

*The Radical Right in Central and Eastern Europe
Since 1989*
Sabrina P. Ramet, ed.

Revolt of the Filmmakers
The Struggle for Artistic Autonomy and the Fall of the
Soviet Film Industry
George Faraday

Russia's Liberal Project
State-Society Relations in the Transition
from Communism
Marcia A. Weigle

THE DENIAL OF BOSNIA

RUSMIR MAHMUTĆEHAJIĆ

Translated by Francis R. Jones and Marina Bowder

Foreword by Ivo Banac

The Pennsylvania State University Press
University Park, Pennsylvania

Library of Congress Cataloging-in-Publication Data

Mahmutćehajić, Rusmir, 1948–
    [Kriva politika: čitanje historije i povjerenje u Bosni English]
    The denial of Bosnia / Rusmir Mahmutćehajić ; translated by Francis R. Jones and
Marina Bowder.

        p.   cm.—(Post-communist cultural studies series)
    Includes bibliographical references and index.
    ISBN 0-271-02030-X (cloth : alk. paper)
    1. Bosnia and Herzegovina—Politics and government—1992–   . 2. Bosnia and
Herzegovina—Historiography.   3. Yugoslav war, 1991–1995—Bosnia and
Herzegovina—Causes.   I. Jones, Francis R., 1955–   . II. Bowder, Marina.
III. Title.   IV. Post-communist cultural studies.
DR1752.M3313 2000
949.74.74203—dc21   99-056307
                                                                                    CIP

Originally published in Sarajevo (Bosnia and Herzegovina) by "DID" Publishing House as
Kriva politika: Čitanje historije i povjerenje u Bosni. Copyright © 1998 by Rusmir
Mahmutćehajić.

English translation copyright © 2000 The Pennsylvania State University
All rights reserved
Printed in the United States of America
Published by The Pennsylvania State University Press,
University Park, PA 16802-1003

It is the policy of The Pennsylvania State University Press to use acid-free paper for the first
printing of all clothbound books. Publications on uncoated stock satisfy the minimum
requirements of American National Standard for Information Sciences—Permanence of
Paper for Printed Library Materials, ANSI Z39.48-1992.

CONTENTS

In one of his early essays, published in the Sarajevo journal *Život* (Life) in 1978, Rusmir Mahmutćehajić wrote about the beginning of his "ascension through the worlds of return to his whole self." That ascension was the task of an entire generation of Bosnian Muslim intelligentsia caught between tradition and modernity, between the promise of socialism and the reality of Communist dictatorship, between the memory of Islamic community and the prospect of Bosniak nationhood. It is therefore not surprising Mahmutćehajić's early work focused on Bosnia's temper—on the discord and dissension that seemed to negate Bosnia's reputation for unity. He tells of Predolje, the ruined township near his native Stolac, in eastern Herzegovina, which he visited "not out of anger, not out of revenge" but in order to see the remnants of a site burned and devastated by insurgent brigands in 1664, during the Candian war. And he tells how these Venetian-backed Uskoks placed sticks through the metal rings on the mosque door to escape from the burning building—"in the absurdity of misunderstood borders, in the absurdity of world divisions, in the impatience of human search, in the flight from the harmony of the world."

It is typical of Mahmutćehajić that he sought legitimate borders within a single indivisible and harmonious world—a world in which the shadow of disunity within individuals and nations will ultimately be lifted and in which all will progress on the way to the Creator. That is why Mahmutćehajić's ascension could not bypass the headstone of a venerable dervish of Predolje, one of the passionate company whose souls do not permit the "dulling of those senses with which we touch the frontiers of the Ocean of love." We have, in short, a search for the roots of the Bosnia that exists beyond the divisions of faith and ideology. Mahmutćehajić, from a family that was on the Partisan side in the nightmare of 1941–45, became a bridge between the world of modern nationhood and eternal faith—the messenger *(vjerovjesnik)* of Bosnia. His language, innocuous to the materialist censor, expressed the reality beyond the massacres, divisions, and even scripture—sacred or profane. Before Mahmutćehajić, Bosniak intellectuals were either secularists of socialist or national orientation, or men of religion, however construed. Mahmutćehajić tried to steer these men of different *Weltanschauungen* into a dialogue. He was ideally placed to do so.

Born in Stolac in June 1948, Rusmir Mahmutćehajić was trained in electrical engineering. He graduated from the University of Sarajevo in 1973, went on to earn a master of science degree (1975) and a Ph.D. (1980) at the University of Zagreb, and continued his specialization at Trieste and Leuven. He administered two institutes at the University of Sarajevo and taught at the University of Osijek, Croatia, from 1985 to 1990. Throughout this period of maturation, Communist authorities subjected him to political harassment. In 1973, under pressure from the secret police, the authorities canceled his scholarship to the University of Clermont-Ferrand. In 1983, at the height of political repression in post-Tito Bosnia, when a group of Bosniak intellectuals headed by Alija Izetbegović was arrested under charges of "counterrevolutionary conspiracy" and "Islamic fundamentalism," Mahmutćehajić was interrogated and his passport was confiscated. Under continued investigation, he could not find employment in his native republic for several years. Indeed, he was a rare intellectual whom the Bosnian Communist authorities unsuccessfully tried to make "cooperative" for more than a decade. This explains his absences from Bosnia-Herzegovina and his university work in Croatia, where he served as dean of the Faculty of Electrical Engineering at the University of Osijek from October 1988 to the beginning of political pluralism in Bosnia-Herzegovina after the November elections of 1990.

Mahmutćehajić was close to Alija Izetbegović, the future founder of the Party of Democratic Action (SDA) and president of Bosnia-Herzegovina, and introduced Izetbegović to the leading Bosniak intellectuals, thereby creating an alliance of religious and national elites. The times were uncertain, and all South Slavic nations were bracing for the onslaught of Slobodan Milošević, who increasingly was turning the League of Communists of Serbia into the party of Serbian nationalism. The high point of Milošević's "anti-bureaucratic revolution" was the overthrow of the party leaderships in Kosovo, Vojvodina, and Montenegro, which he accomplished in 1989. In Bosnia-Herzegovina, too, the federalist leadership of Branko Mikulić and Hamdija Pozderac was under fire. The manufactured "Agrokomerc" affair (1988), which was intended to implicate the Bosnian Communist leadership in the suspect financial dealings of Fikret Abdić, the political and economic boss of northwestern Bosnia, was increasingly seen as an anti-Bosnian ploy that recommended the policy of cohesion for all those who could be won over to an anti-Milošević platform.

By 1989, resistance to Milošević had mounted in the northwestern republics of Slovenia and Croatia. As a result of the systemic collapse of communism throughout Eastern Europe in the fall of 1989, the political arena was opened to the non-Communist forces. The oppositional political parties were legalized during this period, including the oppositional bloc DEMOS in Slovenia, the Croatian Democratic Union (HDZ) of Franjo Tuđman in Croatia, and the Muslim-dominated Party of Democratic Action (SDA) in Bosnia-Herzegovina. At the same time, the final round of Communist republican congresses (November–December 1989) demonstrated the extent to which party was split along republic lines. Although the Bosnian party organization, in which the Serbs played an important role, did not join the Slovenian and Croatian exodus at the last federal party congress in January 1990, its reformed leadership, headed by Nijaz Duraković, placed no obstacles in the way of democratic transition. Precisely at the time when Milošević was countering the HDZ electoral victory in Croatia by fanning the Serb resistance in Croatia's Serb-populated inner rim, Bosnia's multiparty elections (November–December 1990) were won by the anti-Communist national parties: SDA, HDZ, and Radovan Karadžić's SDS. After some wrangling a coalition of these parties established the first post-Communist government of Bosnia-Herzegovina. Although Rusmir Mahmutćehajić was not a member of the SDA, his prestigious position in Bosnia intellectual life was reflected in his appointment to the vice-presidency in the new government.

Bosnia's complex alliance could not be maintained in face of Milošević's war against Slovenia and Croatia. The withdrawal of the Serb-dominated federal army (JNA) from these republics, and its regroupment in Bosnia, boded ill for the republic's tranquillity. The JNA was in control of the vast areas of Bosnia and became the chief arms supplier to Karadžić's para-states, which were cropping up in eastern and northwestern Bosnia and in eastern Herzegovina. In the face of these threats Izetbegović's behavior was uncertain and vacillating. Bosnia was effectively rudderless in face of Great Serbian pressures, which increasingly were coordinated with the pressures of Tuđman's Croatia. The war for creation of nationally homogeneous post-Yugoslav states increasingly was turning into a campaign for the partition of Bosnia.

Bosnia-Herzegovina was faced with a choice: remain in the Serb-dominated rump Yugoslavia, with all the prospects of permanent inequality similar to the status of Kosovo, or opt for independence and the probability of military confrontation with Serbia. This dilemma was resolved in the referendum of 1 March 1992, in which the Bosniak-Croat coalition brought about a pro-independence majority. Serbs, with some exceptions, boycotted the referendum and vowed war. The SDS was already engaged in JNA-sponsored insurgency. By April, at the time of international recognition of Bosnia's independence, the Serb forces commenced an all-out attack along the Drina River frontier, to the Kupres Plateau, and the Sava River valley. The attack was accompanied by unprecedented atrocities, ethnic cleansing, and the construction of concentration camps.

Throughout this period Rusmir Mahmutćehajić was the key strategist of Bosnian independence. Already in April 1991 he was instrumental in establishing the Patriotic League, a multinational force that represented the nucleus of the future Army of Bosnia-Herzegovina (ABH). Without its units and network of contacts, which frustrated the JNA/SDS network, Sarajevo almost certainly would have fallen to the Serb forces in the spring of 1992. Ever alert to anti-Bosnian conspiracies, Mahmutćehajić was steering the Bosnian leadership to resistance. Appointed minister of energetics, mining, and industry in August 1992, he almost single-handedly engaged in the strategic war against the Serbian forces that were strangling the Bosnian capital. Within besieged Sarajevo and elsewhere in Bosnia, he promoted and organized the manufacture of weaponry, frustrating at the same time the Serb military industry in Vogošća. All forces, notably the diplomacies of important powers, that promoted the negotiated settlement of the Bosnian war, which could be accomplished only at the expense of Bosnian unity, had a prominent adversary in Mahmutćehajić. They blamed him for obtaining military help from "wrong countries," as if the "right countries" were not imposing an arms embargo that impeded only one side: the ABH and the internationally recognized Bosnian government. Perhaps this explains why Mahmutćehajić has repeatedly been denied a visa to visit the United States, a sanction that has not been used even against individuals subsequently charged with war crimes.

Milošević's efforts for the conquest and division of Bosnia are well known, and Tuđman's adherence to this policy is no longer news. The tragedy of Bosnia's defense—the essence of the twisted politics, of the *kriva politika* (wrong policy), as Mahmutćehajić has it in the title of the Bosnian edition of this book—is the acceptance of partition by Izetbegović and the SDA. Mahmutćehajić argued more and more with Izetbegović about what he saw as Izetbegović's abandonment of a strong commitment to defense, of the slow slide to the acceptance of partition, of Izetbegović's sponsorship of a Bosniak mini-Bosnia. In June 1993, at the height of Croat atrocities in his native Stolac, whose male Bosniak population was deported to the concentration camps of Dretelj, Gabela, the Mostar Heliodrome, and others, as the Croat authorities proceeded to destroy or bulldoze all Stolac's mosques and Ottoman-style secular buildings, Mahmutćehajić remained strongly opposed to the Owen-Stoletenberg plan for the partition of Bosnia that would have given Stolac to the Bosniak mini-state. His resistance led to a break with Izetbegović. Mahmutćehajić resigned from all his functions in December 1993, determined to pursue the defense of Bosnia rather than support what he considered to be

Izetbegović's malignant idea of defending the "people"—meaning the Bosniaks alone.

The SDA leadership made every effort, dangling the hopes of high positions before Mahmućehajić's, to get him to change his mind, but after the final conversation with Izetbegović, early in 1994, the rift became firm. Mahmućehajić began to pursue his own course and devoted all his energies to restoring trust among Bosnian communities and to fostering dialogue and achieving mutual understanding. The establishment of the International Forum Bosnia (IFB), an organization devoted to the revival of Bosnia's pluralist tradition, crowned these efforts, and Mahmutćehajić became its president in September 1997. The IFB has done an enormous amount to foster dialogue among all parts of fractured Bosnia, and between Bosnia and its neighbors, with Mahmutćehajić personally leading the IFB teams for discussion sessions with the people of the other "entity" (Doboj, "Republika Srpska") and the "Croat part of the Federation" (Livno).

Rusmir Mahmutćehajić sees Bosnia as an abomination to the modern homogenizers, who consciously or unconsciously recognize Bosnia as a residue of an era when humanity was alert to a higher plan at work in temporal and spatial experience. But precisely because the "Bosnian unity in diversity" is based on religious traditions, it is closer to the transcendental sources of justice and can therefore be an example in the universal process of healing. Confronted by Serb and Croat nationalisms, whose function is to foster modern ethnicist exclusiveness, not least of all among the Bosniaks, Bosnia's response must to pursue a steep path. Therefore, the answer is not to accept the modern divisions but to "enter at the narrow gate" (Matthew 7:13) and "scale the Height" (Koran 90:11–12).

The steep path is not relevant to Bosnia alone. Mahmućehajić believes that America's protection of the Bosnian model is actually a huge service on behalf of American-sponsored liberal democracy, which has taken root in European integrations. Contrary to the ignorant claims of Western historians who see the "homogenization of peoples into their own national states as part of a process that, in Europe, has continued uninterruptedly since the time of the French revolution," Mahmutćehajić argues that the opponents of European integration are necessarily anti-Bosnian, anti-liberal, and monist. "The many here are merged in one; one form / Involves the multifarious, thick swarm / (This is the oneness of diversity, / Not oneness locked in singularity)" (Attar).

PREFACE

Since this world's phenomena often occur in dualist forms, the existence of two diametrically opposed concepts of Bosnia and Herzegovina is unsurprising. The first sees Bosnia-Herzegovina as an organic and historic whole; the second holds that the country is a purely artificial creation, the result of a complex historic accident, its parts better off divorced than united. These concepts are paralleled by a dichotomy between two geopolitical master plans, with the balance heavily in favor of the second view of Bosnia.

The first concept, that of Bosnian unity, is commonly associated with an emotional rather than a rational perception of state and society in Bosnia-Herzegovina. The struggle to turn this concept into reality has taken many forms in the churning vortex of Balkan history, but none of them has been strong enough to be decisive.

The opposite concept, that of Bosnia-Herzegovina as an unnatural, nonviable construct, tends to favor the division of the country into two parts, one of which would be annexed to Serbia, the other of which would be annexed to Croatia. This concept is backed by the twin dogmas of Serb and Croat "anti-Bosnianism." The most explicit of its recent manifestations was the Karađorđevo Agreement of 1991, signed by Slobodan Milošević of Serbia and Franjo Tuđman of Croatia, on the division of Bosnia-Herzegovina. The systematic destruction of Bosnia-Herzegovina by war and genocide followed, just as the Serbian and Croatian puppet-masters had agreed. This plan gained its ideological and physical impetus from anti-Bosnian dogma, and was supported by key centers of power in Serbia and Croatia.

By its very nature, this second view of Bosnia-Herzegovina directly conflicts with the existence of a Muslim element in Bosnia-Herzegovina—an element that, according to the advocates of division, is too small and weak to maintain Bosnia-Herzegovina's unity. However, it is also too large to be easily ignored or removed. Therefore the strategy for destroying and dividing Bosnia incorporates a two-pronged attack on the Muslims. The first prong is one of killing, torturing, and ethnic cleansing, combined with the systematic erasure of all evidence of their historic and cultural presence. The second prong is

This is an expanded version of the lecture the author intended to give on 8 June 1997 at Stanford University, "United States Foreign Policy in South-East Europe, from 1989 to 1997." The lecture was never given because the U.S. government refused to grant a visa to the author, who has never personally received an explanation of this refusal.

aimed at diverting their political goal away from the principle of Bosnia-Herzegovina's unity, and driving them toward a vague and ideologized Islamicism—which, of course, finds little favor with the contemporary Western world.

This plan of destruction exploits certain interpretations of history, together with all other means at its disposal, to enable and justify the expansion of Serbia and Croatia. The prime motors of destruction are the anti-Bosnian policies of Belgrade and Zagreb. But they receive extra impetus from a third ally—the forces of "Islamicism" operating within Bosnia-Herzegovina.

The war against Bosnia-Herzegovina, at the start of the final decade of the twentieth century, followed strenuous and persistent "peace" talks, of which the real aim was to carve out new "nation-states" within the territory of Bosnia-Herzegovina. This plan was supported by readings of history obedient to the concept of a reconstituted state divided along "ethnic" lines. Its followers were the ruling oligarchies of Belgrade, represented by Slobodan Milošević; Zagreb, unappetizingly personified by Franjo Tuđman; and Sarajevo, somewhat erratically represented by Alija Izetbegović. These three constitute the unholy trinity of forces working for the destruction of Bosnia-Herzegovina's unity.

This three-way matrix of Bosnia-Herzegovina's destruction has never been systematically analyzed. Usually only one or two of its dimensions have been researched and publicized, depending on which side is viewing it. Meanwhile, the hidden currents surge unchecked. Among the Bosniaks, known to the outside world as "Bosnian Muslims," the destructive forces are seen only as coming from outside, primarily from Serbia and Croatia; the Bosniaks rarely if ever turn their focus inward to inspect their own guilt. Those who pursue this policy of selective blame seem to not realize, or to deliberately ignore, its negative impact on Bosnia-Herzegovina's unity. The prevailing Bosniak interpretation of history and its practical expression in political terms directly or indirectly support the destruction of Bosnia-Herzegovina.

The destruction model outlined above cannot be readily understood unless it is seen in the context of wider European trends. Focusing on the deliberate actions of the destroyers—Serbian, Croatian, and Bosniak—risks only muddying the waters if their role in the threefold matrix is not taken into account. While the three forces are equal in principle, the actual power each possesses is far from equal. Of the Serb, Croat, and Bosniak forces, the first is obviously the more powerful, with its impact more dramatic, than the other two. However, revealing the Bosniak member of this unholy trinity (currently the best hidden of the three) in its proper light could lead, wrongly, to the impression that all three are equal. The actual causes and effects would then lose their proper significance, creating an additional danger for the future of Bosnia-Herzegovina.

The geopolitical future of Europe, which is taking shape through a systematic process of monetary, economic, and political union, presupposes its gradual widening toward the East. This cannot be separated from European-American relations, and the determination of what position Russia is to occupy in Europe's ambitions. This expansion of Europe, in cooperation with America, involves cooperation between widely differing elements on the basis of a common consciousness and joint action for a common future. Bosnia, through currently divided and shaken to its foundations, could act as a model for European progress; if protected, and enabled to develop, Bosnia too could have a place in this brave new world.

However, those working today on behalf of Europe's future have great difficulty finding partners among the political and ideological factions currently dominating Bosnia and its immediate neighbors. Unraveling the Bosnian knot should be part of the process of establishing a new European order. But there is at present no force in Bosnia both strong enough and sufficiently focused on the future to participate actively in this process.

This work will discuss the main dimensions of the matrix of Bosnia-Herzegovina's destruction, starting with the process of destruction itself from 1990 onward. Quotations and descriptions of events, however, are limited by the writer's belief that only publicly attested evidence should be used in forming his conclusions. A wide range of statements and events, known to the writer personally but never publicized, have been omitted from this thesis. However, all evidence that can be reliably verified has contributed to building this model of the anti-Bosnian master plan. The conviction underlying this work is that all accounts of the Bosnia-Herzegovinan catastrophe, one of the worst episodes of human suffering in the contemporary world, should be published in the hope of contributing to a knowledge and understanding of these events. Understanding is the precondition for reconciliation, for the renewal of trust, and for a future of reconstruction and growth.

1

SCHEMING FOR DESTRUCTION

Any study of the events in Bosnia during the final decade of the second Christian millennium will sooner or later reveal the strategies that caused and controlled them. The destroyers of Bosnia prefer to call these events a "civil war" or a "war of religion." Those who see themselves as its defenders usually employ the term "aggression by neighboring states." But any analysis quickly shows that there was a deliberate plan for the annihilation of the country known as Bosnia-Herzegovina.

The strategy as formulated and planned was a highly complex and consistent matrix, which materialized in a torrent of events. Analyzing it is far from easy. However, no positive outcome from the current situation is possible without studying this matrix. Finding out what actually took place in Bosnia is a task of intellectual and moral significance. The chief facts, many of which are now visible to the eye because of the destruction and disintegration they have brought about, must be gathered together and studied as a whole. This will give us a clear understanding of the "destruction model," its achievements, and its future prospects.

The present world order was and is the setting in which these events took place, from the international recognition of Bosnia as a state to its destruction (or, rather, what destruction its destroyers were able to wreak, given the unexpected resistance they encountered). Hence, the matrix underlying these local events should be surveyed and interpreted within the framework of events in the wider world.

The most significant episodes clearly bear witness to an intention to destroy Bosnia with all means at hand, including the erasure of its Bosniak population by means of genocide. Among the most visible effects of this campaign is the fact that Bosniaks today live only in places where they were able to defend themselves (and these places contain far fewer members of the other two nationalities than formerly). Meanwhile, what is left of the mangled Bosnian state survives only because the destroyers were unable to crush the unexpectedly determined resistance put up by those condemned to disappear.

Among the deliberately intended effects was the destruction of all explicitly Bosnian values as embodied in traditional concepts and practices. This was to be accompanied by the creation and propagation of non-Bosnian or anti-Bosnian concepts and practices. The intended result was that Bosnia as a state should be seen as relevant to only one "faction," thus justifying the mutilation and dismemberment of Bosnia-Herzegovina.

The reorganization of Europe at the end of the Second World War was inspired by a simplistic model of multiplicity and diversity. Then, with the onset of the Cold War, the forces ranged against ideological totalitarianism looked for allies among those traditional elements that have always put up a strong resistance to change. Thus outsiders, dissidents, and opposition groups in the Communist world generally centered their resistance on traditionalist values. These were usually connected with a particular (often religious) denomination, which usually had little or no focus on nonsectarian, transcendent values. Thus, many dubious ideologies, fundamentally incompatible with the democratic or liberal ideals usually seen as "pro-European," received explicit or implicit encouragement from the West. These ideologies were encouraged, or at least tolerated, because they were perceived as more acceptable than the Communist establishment, and as strong and cohesive enough to act as a stable sub-

---

1. *Bosnia: A Country Handbook, Peace Implementation Force (IFOR)*, DOD-1540-17-96, May 1996, 4-1. This handbook was produced as a joint undertaking by many organizations within the U.S. Department of Defense: the Defense Intelligence Agency, the Marine Corps Intelligence Agency, the National Ground Intelligence Center, the National Air Intelligence Center, the Joint Analysis Center of the United States European Command, the 480th Air Intelligence Group, Armed Forces Medical Intelligence Center, and the Missile and Space Intelligence Center.

2. The quote in *Bosnia: A Country Handbook* actually reads: "The Croats, settling a broad crescent of land from Dalmatia along the Adriatic through Croatia and Slavonia, established their own kingdom under Tomislav in 924, but soon fell under the domination of other rulers: Byzantine, Hungarian, Venetian, French, and Austrian" (ibid., 4-1–4-2). The claim concerning the establishment of Tomislav's Kingdom in 924 is treated as an indisputable fact, although we find this concept of a coronation having taken place on the Duvno Field for the first time in Ivana Kukuljević Sakcinski (1816–89). Sakcinski is used by a source that titles itself *The Chronicle of the Priest of Dioclea*, or, more correctly, *The Slav Kingdom*, in which an anonymous chronicler from Bar describes an assembly at which a ruler named Svatopluk was

stitute. This connivance is the key to many of the causes and consequences of the Bosnia-Herzegovina genocide.

In *Bosnia: A Country Handbook,* produced by the American military service, a short summary of local history is introduced: "In the Balkans, past history is closely linked with perceptions of the present and future. Religious and cultural animosities have developed over centuries, and are deeply ingrained among the various warring factions. Violence has been, and will likely continue to be, prevalent."[1]

This historical summary, highly revealing where contemporary misunderstandings of the relationships between peoples and states in this region of the Balkans are concerned, concentrates almost exclusively on two medieval phenomena: the Kingdom of Croatia, established in the tenth century,[2] and the Tsardom of Serbia, which reached its peak in the fourteenth century.[3] In this particular reading of history, there is no mention of any medieval Bosnian state. The promotion of Serb and Croat statehood takes place, by implication, at the expense of Bosnian statehood. Henry Kissinger, on another occasion, reinforced this denial of Bosnia with the following statement: "There was never a Bosnian state on the current territory of Bosnia."[4] The only mention accorded to the Bosniaks in the context of this alleged "Kingdom of the Croats" and "glorious Serb Tsardom" was that they "converted to Islam in great numbers while under Turkish rule."[5]

This example, highly revealing for the image of Bosnia it promotes, implies a logical matrix with three dimensions. The first dimension is that the contemporary Croatian state and its ethno-national policy maintain an unbroken link with the medieval Croat state. The second is that the contemporary Serb state and its ethno-national policy have unbroken ties with the medieval Orthodox state. The third reduces Bosniak ethno-national policy to that of a group that divorced itself from its origins by its choice of an "incompatible" religion. No other option is given. In this matrix it follows that Serb and Croat politics form

---

crowned in a field named Dalma. For details, see Neven Budak and Vladimir Posavac, *Rađanje suvremene Hrvatske i Europe* [The birth of contemporary Croatia and Europe] (Zagreb, 1997).

3. *Bosnia,* 4-2: "The Serb Tsardom reached its greatest glory under Stefan Dušan in the fourteenth century."

4. H. A. Kissinger, "Limits To What the U.S. Can Do in Bosnia," *Washington Post,* 22 September 1997, A19.

5. *Bosnia,* 4-2. For consideration of what follows, it is important that the reader remember the original meaning of the English verb *to convert:* the Latin root is *convertere* (to turn oneself, to turn oneself toward), compounded from *con* (together, jointly) and *vertere* (to turn). The basic meanings are "to turn," "to change," "to turn into a different substance or shape," "to transform," "to shift from one faith, teaching, thinking, direction or action to another," and so on.

part of a continuous and recognizable process of self-determination, while Bosniak politics cannot make the same claim.

Though not obvious at first glance, the interpretation that inspired the Dayton Agreement is closely related to this view of the three protagonists. This agreement divided Bosnia into two constitutional entities: the Federation of Bosnia-Herzegovina, which covers 51 percent of Bosnia-Herzegovina's territory, and the Republika Srpska, which covers 49 percent. The Washington Agreement, which laid the foundations of the Federation and preceded Dayton by almost two years, specified that the Federation should form special "confederal" relations with the Republic of Croatia. Not long after the signing of the Dayton Peace Agreement, the Republika Srpska signed an agreement on special relations with the rump Yugoslavia, now consisting of Serbia and Montenegro. At the end of 1997, the Republic of Croatia issued a proposal for "special relations" with the Federation. The relations proposed could be interpreted as involving the direct incorporation of this part of Bosnia-Herzegovina in the Republic of Croatia.[6]

Thus the current state of Bosnia-Herzegovina was, so to speak, deliberately set up in order to be parceled out between two powers: the Croat and Serb states, ideological successors to "Tomislav's Kingdom" and "Dušan's Tsardom."

Systematically identifying the elements that form the basis of today's Bosnia-Herzegovina is therefore a task that is crucial to Bosnia's future. Thus far, rational solutions have been imposed on phenomena that are significantly deeper and more complex than the rational model conveys, suggesting that the apparent halting of the destructive tide may be only illusory. Meanwhile, the same internal forces remain present, waiting to burst out again in a new guise, with perhaps even greater strength than before.

6. This demand represents the culmination of the model that Tuđman, at the beginning of 1992, sketched out in a message of advice to a Bosnian Croat leader: "You must always demand the same as the Serbs are demanding. But you should do this after them." This was his answer to the question of what position the Croat representatives should take on Cutileiro's proposal to divide Bosnia into three ethno-national states.

2

"Tomislav's Kingdom" and "Dušan's Tsardom," as mentioned in the *Handbook,* are two typical medieval European states. They were ruled in typical medieval European style, with rapid changes of dynasties, alliances, and borders. In a wider historic context they are hardly of major significance, being only two out of dozens of such entities from the Balkan region. Modern-day readings of them are, however, based on the post–Cold War trend of establishing a series of ethnic nation-states in southeastern Europe. This desire to build new nation-states is the successor to the "imperialist drive," which in turn took over the long-standing campaign of the Austro-Hungarian Empire and its allies to rid Europe of Turkish military and political presence.

   All developments that took place in the Balkan region after it came into contact with Islam were viewed as consequences of, and therefore comparable to, this Turkish presence. Thus, strategies for eliminating the Turkish military and political presence from Europe were often accompanied by strategies for eliminating Muslims from the continent, by conversion or expulsion. Moreover, the schemes for building new states out of the ruins of the Turkish Empire were ideologically grounded in the concept of Europe as a Christian continent and Islam as the chief enemy of Christendom. They all incorporated a strong distinction between "Us" and "Them." The national "Us" became identified, in Serbia and Croatia, with the lost, idealized "Tomislav's Kingdom" and "Dušan's Tsardom," founded on Christianity and the whole of human virtue.

"They" were non-Christian, the forces of evil, the enemies of virtue. Love for the ethno-national "Us" is proportional in strength to the hatred of "Them." The sense of moral superiority accompanying the calls for absolute ethnic and national dominance is manifest in the savagery used against those perceived to be in opposition to "Us."

For example, all of history can be interpreted to confirm the image of "Us" as true and proper Christians, enslaved and robbed of all rights, and "Them" as the enslavers and robbers, as dirty, evil Muslims. The battle "We" are fighting for recognition has as its ultimate goal total victory over "Them." This war for Christendom is accompanied by a general perception that it is being fought on behalf of all that is good in the human spirit.

Since the "Others" are Muslims, Christianity and Islam are seen as incompatible, irreconcilable opposites. This contention is drawn not from the principles of Christianity itself, but from a set of historic events, all of which make up an ideologized, secular matrix of history, into which Christianity is subsequently woven.[1] The process is adjusted, by external tailoring, to suit the faction or sect in question. Religion is thus divorced from transcendent principles of tolerance or charity and converted into a tool of ethno-nationalist ideology. For any understanding of Balkan events, it is important to note how often interpretations of religion coincide with nationalist ideologies, and the strong correspondence between religious and ethno-national establishments. To understand the method by which Bosnia-Herzegovina's unity was destroyed, we need to examine the nature of contemporary sectarianism.

1. This model pervades even contemporary geostrategic views of the future world order. Zbigniew Brzezinski expresses it as follows: "Although at this stage the ultimate eastern limits of Europe can neither be defined firmly nor finally fixed, in the broadest sense Europe is a common civilization, derived from the shared Christian tradition. Europe's narrower Western definition has been associated with Rome and its historical legacy. But Europe's Christian tradition has involved also Byzantium and its Russian Orthodox emanation." Zbigniew Brzezinski, *The Grand Chessboard: American Primacy and Its Geostrategic Imperatives* (New York, 1997), 81.

The claim made above is correct but not complete. Europe could follow a completely Christian model only if it were completely Christian. The claim, one based solely on weight of numbers, excludes the Muslim and Jewish elements. Therefore, Jews and Muslims easily became the "Others" of Europe, thus confounding the principles of Christianity. This would be the case even if Judaism and Islam were holy teachings present only in parts of the world distant from Europe. But these three demonstrations of one and the same truth are not divisible, and their inheritors do not live only alongside one another but among one another. This is summed up in Christ's words: "You will love the Lord your God with all your heart, with all your soul, with all your mind and all your strength; you shall love your neighbor as yourself. This is the first and the greatest commandment. And the second is like unto it, You shall love your neighbor as yourself. On these two commandments hang all the law and the prophets" (Matthew 22:37–40). Accordingly, if Europe is not also seen as Jewish and Muslim, it cannot really be Christian. But today the question of the communal values of humanity in the world as a whole remain largely unanswered. How, for example, in the construction of the new world, can relationships and dialogue take place between Christianity and Islam, Confucianism, Buddhism, and the like?

The image of Europe as the "Continent of Christendom" bestows a sacred quality on European culture. This quality has undergone many changes on the long road via Communist atheism to post-Communist ethno-national religiosity.

The Bosnian concept of God as Unity has manifested itself in a diversity of forms: all forms see God as One, and in their diversity bear witness to the Unity of God. But when forms start to see themselves as essence, they become an end in themselves. Godliness is discarded, and atheism adopted in its place. Although the most explicit form of atheism as an ideology is Communism, atheism is more widespread and varied. It lies at the heart of the dogma of religious elites and behind ideologies that bear a superficial appearance of religiousness. The religious content of such ideologies is carefully structured and packaged into a single ideological form. This places the ideology in opposition to every form that is not in perfect agreement with it, which means the loss of essential or transcendent religious truths—and thus worship of the chosen form implies hatred and denial of others.

When devotion to outward form loses sight of inner essence, the ideologies and organizations involved are also cut off from this inner essence, although they keep the appearance of sanctity. This is one of the most dangerous phenomena of our time: religious forms irreligious beneath the surface, gleefully attacking Communism in the sacred name of religion, obsessed with surface but divorced from the core.

People are thus forced to kowtow to a host of worthless manifestations—and to those behind them who hold the reins. The power of the so-called Communist establishment has been shaken to its foundations, and in many countries it has been broken. Many of the recent phenomena in the South Slav lands cannot be explained without taking into account this move from a Communist, atheist mentality to a mentality of new ideologies clothed in the semblance of sanctity. One ideology has simply been exchanged for another, which may be significantly more dangerous than the first. Both ignore the essence: externals rank far higher in their books than inner life. Evil has merely been exchanged for evil.

Political ideologies formed in such a manner always use the Other's guilt as their line of defense. But this guilt is highly elastic it has to stretch down the whole course of history, for the aim is to prove that today's political utopia would have been handed down intact from the Middle Ages—had it not been for the Other's interference, of course. Thus the blurred and ambiguous shapes left by history are metamorphosed into ideologically-polished holy relics, slotted into the logic of contemporary thinking, and blurred with rose-tinted visions of history. "We," of course, cannot be guilty: at the heart of this type of political ideology usually lies the fundamental conviction that God is made in man's image.

The image of the medieval Croatian state is the bulwark of Croatia's current political strategy: its exact counterpart is the image of the ideal Serbian state. However, the territories of these kingdoms, both of which are seen as covering large tracts of Bosnian territory, are inconveniently overlapping. Their interpretations of their historical presence in Bosnia-Herzegovina and their alleged right to resume their former hegemonies are mutually exclusive. But both would agree in basing their denial of Islam and the rights of its followers on their own self-image as defenders of Christendom. Muslims have no place in this vision.

This vision was put into effect in 1939, in the articles of the Cvetković-Maček Agreement, which divided Bosnia-Herzegovina into "Serb" and "Croat" municipalities. The division was to be made on the basis of the number of Serbs or Croats each region contained, regardless of how many Muslims there might be. From this it could be deduced that the latter had no existence, or would soon have none.

In 1991, the partition of Bosnia-Herzegovina was redrafted by the Serb and Croat ruling elites. Comparison of these maps shows no disputed territory, and no Muslim population. The Muslims, eliminated on paper but nevertheless present, were the main obstacle to the plan and therefore the enemy of both ethno-national elites.

3

THE CHRISTIAN MODEL OF EUROPE

In speaking of Tomislav's Kingdom and Dušan's Tsardom as historical precedents for the contemporary nation-states of the Croats and Serbs, we need to discuss their religious differences, which they have preserved from the medieval model until today. Tomislav's Kingdom has crucial links with Roman Catholicism, and Dušan's Tsardom with Orthodoxy. The relationship between these two versions of Christianity, the ancient schism between them, and the possibilities of bridging the gulf have had a crucial impact on latter-day South Slav history.

Catholicism and Orthodoxy are founded on the same holy scriptures. Thus they cannot be called separate religions. The oldest preserved form of the New Testament, in the ancient Greek, is the source for both churches' understanding of Christ. The difference between them arose initially in their interpretation of the Testament. This disagreement might therefore be resolved by returning to the sources or, as today's ecumenical movement often asserts, by adopting the apostolic concept of the church as unity expressed through multiplicity.

Contemporary liberal democracy cannot be separated from its Christian heritage, and its history suggests a built-in evangelical desire to overcome all its internal differences and ultimately encompass the entire world. The question of finally uniting these varied interpretations of the Christian source is increasingly being raised in the contemporary Western world. The host of different churches today, based on a host of different interpretations of the same scriptures, can and must be united. Normalizing the relationship between the Catholic and the Orthodox churches is of prime importance for such an undertaking. The disagreement between the two churches is seen as a temporary phenomenon, which can be overcome by focusing awareness on their underlying unity.

This approach can be seen in many current political ideologies. Bringing the countries of Eastern Christianity back beneath the wing of Western civilization, from which they were excluded by a series of unfortunate accidents in the past, and more recently by Communist rule, is seen as a key task of contemporary ecumenicalism. This ambition is closely linked with spreading the ideology of liberal democracy.

In today's ethno-national politics, this is shown by a desire for a good relationship with the established churches. This phenomenon, taken by itself, is normally interpreted as a return to religious values after the long and unnatural division imposed by the atheistic ideology of the Communist establishment. But here a deep human need is being exploited by a cynically rationalistic political drive to manufacture past and present self-justifications by exploiting contemporary trends of Western thought. This underlies every act of the ruling political ideologies in Croatia and Serbia. Disagreements and conflicts are perceived as freak phenomena, opposed to the "essence" of nationhood. This image of nationhood is always presented as being in harmony with the fundamentals of Western civilization and therefore in tune with the development of Europe today.

The Croats (as Catholic Christians) and the Serbs (as Orthodox Christians) are both eager to declare that their ethno-national policies are in harmony with historical trends and the current world order. The schism between Catholicism and Orthodoxy, accordingly, is no deeper or more significant than the ethno-national divide between the states of the Croats and the Serbs. (Nor should the common denominator of the hidden but still-powerful Communist elements in the ruling establishments of these two states be forgotten.) [1]

1. The most important loci of the relations under discussion are the Serb, Croat, and Bosniak nations. All three are equal in principle but not in age and strength. The concept of the Serb nation developed in accordance with similar trends in Europe during the eighteenth and nineteenth centuries. This phenomenon was followed by the birth of "Croat nationhood." In view of these circumstances, the Muslim or "Bosniak" element presents a series of obstacles that are not acceptable to Serbian and Croatian aspirations. Therefore, the Bosniaks are viewed as raw material for one or the other of the two plans. Bosnia's multiplicity of sacred traditions is opposed to such ideological plans by its very nature, and thus "lags behind" the aspirations of its neighbors. This is particularly obvious in the case of the movement known today as as "Bosniak." The Communist promotion of the "national question" as a force that could provide support for its own ideological worldview was taken up by more recent ethno-national trends, which added ideological elements of their own. Therefore, it is important to point out that the current Serb, Croat, and Bosniak national ideologies contain many Communist elements. Regardless of external

Although this gives us a clear model for relationships between the two countries, the absence of neat borders between the two sides (whose separation, according to the model, is a matter of historic necessity) becomes a burning issue. And Muslims are the obstacle. Their presence is viewed as an historic anomaly incompatible with the self-proclaimed advance of the other two nations toward the promised land of liberal democracy. Bosnia-Herzegovina is the geographic expression of this anomaly. Within its borders, Muslims, Orthodox Christians, and Catholic Christians are so intermingled that it is impossible to draw neat borders between them. The only answer is to explain the presence of Islam as the artificial result of "mass conversion." Since the Muslims were converted, so the advocates of partition claim, they must have originally belonged to one side or the other. Had there been no such "mass conversion," this theory urges, clear borders would now exist between the Serb and Croat territories and peoples. Within the framework of contemporary ecumenicalism, this would enable the establishment of a "proper" relationship between the two states, one based on religious unity.

The "conversion" of the Bosniaks to Islam therefore remains a highly unhelpful anomaly. It is seen as wholly different, of course, from pagan Europe's conversion to Orthodox or Catholic Christianity. The fact of conversion to Islam and the presence of Islamic culture is unacceptable and runs counter to the explicit and implicit content of nationalist ideology: that of a steady advance toward internationally recognized, comprehensive mono-ethnic states able to take their rightful place in the European Union. The Muslim presence clashes, in this scenario, with the development of liberal-democratic principles; thus, it is the alleged duty of "true" Christians to remove this anomaly.

Contemporary nationalist ideology tries to ally itself as far as possible with the churches, so that a single concept of faith may cover the whole region. At the core of religion lies man's search for God in himself, as a being created in the likeness of God. Face to face with the ultimate source of creation, in his relationship with himself and the outside world, man has a choice between betraying himself and validating himself. The first involves isolating himself from the source of perfection; this is often accompanied by focusing hatred on others. The second involves uncovering the self, and searching for and recognizing the internal elements of perfection in the self and in others. These two aspects of human behavior have clashed throughout history.

Struggles for "national" recognition are in keeping with the ideology of the

---

changes, philosophical approaches to the national question remain largely Communist in nature. This situation will probably continue, in spite of the fact that religious structures are becoming more and more deeply involved in the process.

contemporary age. Blaming the Other and waging war on them enables Us to achieve self-determination and liberation. The national ideologies that are out to destroy the concept of Bosnia-Herzegovina are agreed in regarding the Muslims as the ultimate Other. The Muslims are the guilty party—guilty, among other "crimes," of depriving the Croats and Serbs of the freedom to create ethnically pure nation-states founded on liberal-democratic principles, and thus to become prime candidates for membership in the European Union.

History, especially in the last two centuries, has tended to be theorized in terms of coherent, directed progress. Although not always following a straight line, it is usually seen as reaching its end or climax around whichever period the historian is writing in. This climax is seen as resolving the internal conflicts that have influenced the course of history from its "primitive" beginnings to the "advanced" state in which humanity now finds itself, that is, from traditional to modern social conditions. This theory holds that the principles and institutions of the present social order have reached such a state of evolution that there can no longer be any more significant developmental changes.

"The climax of history" was defined by Hegel as the liberal state and by Marx as the communist state. Two ideologies grew out of these definitions: liberal democracy and socialism. Their opposition has colored the entire twentieth century. The ruling establishments founded on these ideologies succeeded in stopping and destroying Nazism, but created the Iron Curtain. The division between them spanned the globe. The confidence of their fin-de-siècle supporters in the coming of "the end of history" in the form of the ideal society was dented by the horrors of the First World War, Hitlerism, Stalinism, and the Second World War. These events and many of their consequences resulted in considerable disillusionment as to the inevitable march of progress: atrocities on such an unprecedented scale were possible *because* of "civilization," not in spite of it. Evil became banality, and pessimism the accepted worldview.

Then the unexpected and total collapse of the "Communist world" began. Suddenly the internal weaknesses of the system were evident to all. The perceived superiority of the liberal-democratic world contributed to the disintegration of the dualist structure of the Cold War. Belief in universal historical progress gained force again. The collapse of systems based on Communist ideologies and the obvious prosperity of those founded on liberal democracy and free markets formed an environment in which models of "universal history" could flourish once more.

The indisputable progress of postindustrial scientific development contributed to this optimistic model. While industrial and scientific development does not necessarily require a liberal democratic society, the nonliberal democratic states were less able to handle the complexities of postindustrialism, including the spread of information technology and the mass media. A simplistic rationalization of individual and group activity that reduced humanity to the desire for unlimited material gain was clearly inadequate when it came to rationalizing all of human behavior. A liberal-democratic environment, which offered individuals and groups a greater degree of personal fulfillment, proved more successful in satisfying the three elements of the human soul as defined by Plato: Desire, Reason, and Thymos.

The first two aspects, material satisfaction and the increase of knowledge, underpin economic theories of humanity's desire for unlimited gain. But the fall of the Communist world (which was admittedly hastened by economic problems) demonstrated the existence of a human need beyond what can be satisfied by good economics. The desire for freedom, which the liberal state apparently encourages and fulfills, can be linked to Thymos.

The recently rejuvenated theory of universal history centers precisely on this element: that liberal democracy enables the satisfaction of Thymos, which socialism ignores and suppresses. Thymos can express itself as desire for recognition. Man wishes to be recognized and acknowledged as having individual dignity and value. This need can outweigh those desires that can be met by good economics. The Communist system collapsed because it failed to realize the significance of this need. Communism provided industrialization, improved living conditions, and mass education, but it did nothing for Thymos.

Liberal democracy is seen, by contrast, as meeting this need. Dissatisfaction with Communism led to self-proclaimed movements toward liberal democracy. Liberal-democratic observers identified this as a natural longing for recognition, above all for "national," religious, and cultural distinctions. Thus the Western world viewed with sympathy the struggles of Croatia and Serbia for clearly defined national borders within which their own traditions, cultures, and religions could reign supreme. And so the international community found it difficult to understand why Bosnia's problems could not be solved by negotiating similar borders around all three of its "peoples."

4

A THIRD HISTORY

The fall of the Communist bloc and the collapse of its ruling system was fatal to Yugoslavia, the country cobbled together in 1918 out of several distinct historical and cultural entities. Yugoslavia's fall has been interpreted as the outcome of the inherent incapacity of the Communist system to meet spiritual needs, including the desire for "recognition." But this desire for general recognition was reinterpreted, in the frame of ethno-national ideologies, as the freedom to impose on others, willy-nilly, their own demands for "recognition" and "rights." The result was a paradoxical denial of liberalism, if liberal democracy is understood as guaranteeing general and mutual recognition for all. Such a denial is not unusual during the transition from Communism to "liberal democracy" and has the potential to produce tyranny far greater than that of Communism. Religion and ethnicity often play central roles in this drama. Paradoxically again, they provide the motivation for conflict but also the potential to create a society genuinely founded on liberal-democratic principles of tolerance and dialogue.

Campaigns to win ethno-national recognition by force while explicitly or tacitly denying the equality of other nationalities, cultures, and religions were supported by readings of history that stressed the worth of one nation, and its culture and religion, at the expense of others. These readings are at the core of anti-Bosnianism. Liberal democratic society has partially succeeded in reconciling the recognition of one particular nationality or religion with the recognition of others. To date, however, it has not had to tackle a society as complex and interwoven as Bosnia-Herzegovina's, where Muslims, Catholics, and Orthodox have lived together for centuries in roughly equal proportions: hence any interpretation of the Bosnian drama inevitably includes readings of history containing a host of time-worn prejudices about the Muslims and their relationships with Christians.

Christianity and Islam both regard themselves as comprehensive holy teachings. They consider themselves a means by which God has laid down a way of life and faith applicable to all people, to be carefully passed down and preserved through time. For this reason, the notion of a relationship between them requires that they should be perceived as transcending national ideologies. The Bosnian-Herzegovinan model of tolerance and inter-religious relationships can be interpreted as accepting that all religion should enable the reunion of all human beings with their single transcendent origin.

This acceptance could be worded in a religious context as follows. God is the ultimate creator in every holy tradition. There is no creator besides Him, for all people are His creations. He reveals His path through His prophets, who proclaim the same universal essence in different ages and to different peoples. The criteria by which members of an individual religion define their choice as all-encompassing cannot exclude the truth of the revelations of other faiths. No holy teaching can retain its claim to universality if it denies the right of others to follow another road; nor, however, must the fact be denied that their interpretations of the sacred sources may differ.

On this basis it is possible not only to acknowledge but to rejoice in the differences between the Christian churches, the different interpretations of the Koran and the Prophet Muhammad among Muslims, the various sects of Judaism, and so on. These differences neither deny the underlying Unity nor diminish the possibility of salvation for their followers. All human history upholds this variety and the search for Unity in multiplicity. However, where there is no cultural tradition of seeing Unity in such differences, or where this tradition is denied, multiplicity crystallizes into hostile groups gathered around separate leaders. Such groupings are inevitably accompanied by a denial of other groups. But if the Bosnian model teaches us that diversity can co-exist with Unity, it should be possible to appreciate all individual desires and ways of approaching Unity. Every attempt to reach Unity should, at the same time, bring one closer to others who express the same yearning in different ways.

Truth is universal, and all manifestations dwell in the Truth. But it cannot be diverted toward one and away from another: it is supra-individual. All interpretations of Truth from an individual standpoint are relative; it cannot be the exclusive property of one interpretation, one manifestation. It cannot be dependent on any individual time, region, or language. Truth is the key element of all individuality and is linked to all individuality. Each individuality can only have meaning through its relationship to Truth. Truth is the source and center of Unity. Ignoring this principle reduces Truth to the level of interpretation and turns content into mere form, showing itself in contemporary society as sectarianism and confessionalism.

In this context, Bosnian history in all its manifestations can be understood as a belief that the three main religious routes can and should be seen in relationship to Unity, to their common origin. This mission is expressed by the words of the message: "Dispute not with the People of the Book, save in the fairer manner, except for those of them that do wrong; and say, 'We believe in what has been sent down to us, and what has been sent down to you; our God and your God is One, and to Him we have surrendered!' " (Koran 29:46). This belief has never achieved full expression in explicit policy terms, but it is deeply rooted in people's perception of the world. The interweaving of different holy forms is a local fact of life. But their inter-relationship is not only an effect of place, time, and the ebb and flow of geopolitics. It can also be linked to the transcendent capacity of religion itself. But current political trends are incapable, for the most part, of recognizing the organic links between the different religious teachings in Bosnia-Herzegovina.

Plans for marking out the territories of the Serb and Croat states are accompanied by a stern denial of any transcendent relationship between the heirs of Catholicism, Orthodoxy, and Islam. The two chief nationalist ideologies, Serb and Croat, whatever their view of each other, share a common view of Islam. Both link the Bosniaks to a vision of Islam whose founding principle is an anti-Bosnian one. The Bosniaks are reproached for their adherence to Islam but are simultaneously denied any "third history" of their own by tales of their "mass conversion" from Orthodoxy or Catholicism. As a reaction, the Bosnian Muslims are driven to adopt a sectarian or confessionalist attitude to Islam. Thus the universality of religion is reduced to the individualities of interpretations, symbols, and ideas, the differences become unbridgeable, and all individual sects and faiths deny all relationship with each other. In such a way, a complex historical space is reduced to three "histories": Serb, Croat, and Bosniak. Since the first two are linked to forms of Christianity, the denial of differences between them can be seen as an integral component of a wider campaign to promote liberal democracy as a universal value. But there is little rationale for the exclusion of the third on the same basis.

Here, therefore, we see a sustained effort to turn distinct religious world-views, linked to separate languages and separate religious communities, into the tools of ethno-national strategies. The fundamentals of the Serb Orthodox church are "obviously" indistinguishable from the Serb ethno-national plan. In this concept of Christianity there is no higher value than the spiritualized goals of the ethno-national plan. A similar trend is apparent in the Croatian Catholic Church, though its incompatibility with world Catholicism as a whole is evident throughout the history of both the Croatian Church and the Croatian ethno-national plan.

The "third history" of the three, however, is opposed to the other two, since it is part of a civilization generally seen as out of harmony with the principles of liberal democracy and Christianity. In response, this third history must, as its basic proposition, devote itself to the same process of allocating blame that forms the founding principle of the Serb and Croat versions of history. The Bosniak version shows the same need to justify the distinction between Us and Them. In so doing, it has left the principle that "Your God and Our God is One" far behind. There are plenty of well-documented examples of this sectarian denial of the shared principles of religious faith in the promotion of Bosniak exclusivity. "The members of all religions," says a contemporary Bosniak writer, "mark the word God with a capital G, and this use of the noun God to represent Allah fails to recognize the distinction between Allah and the godheads of other religions, which is the fundamental point of Islam."[1] This is a sad example of how the universality of religion is explicitly denied in favor of a new sectarianism.

In such a way, the relationships between holy teachings are reduced, for political reasons, to a reading of scriptures that emphasizes their incompatibility. But because there is a wealth of arguments inherent in each teaching that obliges its followers to respect the sacred nature of every other teaching, such readings can be refuted and overturned by the intellectual efforts of those who rebel against politics as a means of forcing one's will upon another.

1. E. Duraković, *O nekim značajnim prevodilačkim pogreškama* [Concerning certain significant errors by translators], (1417/18 H.G.) (Sarajevo, 1996), 35.

5

EXCLUSIVENESS AND UNIVERSALITY

Humanity has one incontestable right—the right to redemption. This right is not limited by time or place, by race or language, by religion or material power. It bears witness to the holiness of humanity as God's creation. Redemption reaches out to every individual but is independent of the world of individual forms. It can be seen as independent of humanity, while humanity depends on it totally. Every individual looks toward redemption according to the disposition with which each is created. The nature of human freedom lies in this disposition, which reveals the seeds of perfection in each being. But this movement toward perfection differs from individual to individual. It is individual and universal at one and the same time. It is individual because it never takes the same shape twice, from one individual to another, but it is universal because there is no redemption without the Redeemer, the One and Only Perfection.

This explains why there are many religions, and the significance of repeatedly forging links with Unity or Truth cannot be overemphasized. The stronger and the more decisive a human being's attachment to the transcendent unity of redemption, the clearer all the different forms of insight into the source of perfection and into his or her potential to reestablish these links and the more valid the effort of each individual.

If this claim is applied to the Bosnian model, then it must be acknowledged that the religions of Christians and Muslims share this same unconditional, simultaneous individuality and universality. To be a Christian means, in the message Christianity incorporates, to acknowledge the ways by which others move toward the Absolute, which is unconditionally universal. From this it follows that every being and every different form of seeking—of which there are literally as many as there are individual beings—is created for this universality. All holy teachings, in all their multiplicity, are reliable ways of seeking, proclaiming, and bearing witness to "the opening of Heaven."

"The opening of Heaven" is uniquely expressed and acknowledged in the diversity of the sacred teachings incorporated in the Bosnian model. It is present when individuals acknowledge their shared nature. It demonstrates the presence of the supra-individual and supra-formal world, the source of fulfillment for all human potential in this world of individual forms. The minarets, spires, domes, and Stars of David in our towns testify to this truth, as does the mingling of church bells with the call of the muezzin. The tolerance manifest in this multiple presence of individual creeds bears witness to the universal nature of human redemption. The existence of this tolerance in Bosnia is possible only if the forms of holy tradition do not deny the universal and sacred nature of humankind.

History, however, is not exactly overcrowded by examples of the capacity of individuals and communities to acknowledge each other's worth. Whenever a form of individuality or community—no matter what its national, religious, political, or other orientation may be—is cut off from universality, it ceases to be aware that every human being is holy. The Other then becomes an inconvenient obstacle to "Our" exclusivity. Religion loses its basic principle, that of renewing the union with Being. Instead, it shrinks to a collection of preserved heirlooms and memories. These are fiercely defended against anybody seen as having no connection with the feelings they generate. In this passionate defense of the old and cherished heirlooms of one's great ancestors, humanity itself is often forgotten and discarded. And the Other becomes hated with a bitter energy in order to prove one's adherence to these inherited values.

The existence of a multitude of ways to seek redemption is consequently seen as negative, and the claim that something other than the one and only "correct" expression of the sacred truth exists is seen as a falsehood. The Franciscan friars, the Mawlawi dervishes, and the Orthodox monks are all different in the expression of their unique feeling for the Essence and in their unique way of seeking it, and they are all holy. But if the awareness of what lies above and beyond them is lost, their holiness disappears as external forms assume priority. And all today's misbegotten economic, ideological, and political schemes are rushing to exploit and exacerbate this act of forgetting.

Recent events point to a sad inability to let respect for the individual and the universal nature of faith prevail over politics. The destructive frenzy of exclusivity is surely the worst advertisement for those interpretations of faith that are used to justify the frenzy. To suggest that separation of communities according to religion is the solution is to claim that religion promotes hatred more successfully than it promotes tolerance. The only constructive answer is to initiate dialogue between all members of Bosnia's unity in diversity. This dialogue is most urgently needed between those who justify their exclusivity on the basis of holy teachings, since these are the ones who give the strongest support to the evil elites, ideologies, and organizations and the perpetrators of crimes that they generate. The expulsions and killings, the defiling and destroying of places of worship, and the desecration of graves should cause all who respect the sacred nature of holy teachings to unite in opposition. For them to be silent and fail to condemn represents a betrayal worse than the original act, which was committed by those who believed that religion stood firmly behind them.

6

By "ecumenism" is meant the Church's awakened consciousness of its universal elements and the arousal of its sense of calling and service. It is a movement toward Church unity. Its nature and significance in the twentieth century spring partly from the Christian desire for a greater and more effective role in the events of the contemporary world. The beauty of faith as experienced by the true Christian is marred by the ugliness of church division and by the frequent hostility between churches and their various peoples. This discord can be overcome, the promoters of ecumenism believe, by investigating and proclaiming the pure apostolic message, by which the Church is recognized as *to soma Christou,* the body of Christ. Differences between spiritual heritages, in this view, should no longer be a cause for division and opposition, and examining the beliefs of different churches will lead to a strengthening of ecumenical feelings and an understanding of historic differences. The healing of the deep wounds of schism, inflicted throughout ancient and medieval history, can be achieved, according to the ecumenists, by promoting an ecumenical theology. This will involve reexamining the real nature and meaning of the legacy of theological and ecclesiastic writings in the light of what is considered to be historic truth.

This undertaking does not involve Islam, although its exclusion is a betrayal of its very foundation and universal goals. If the multitude of Christian churches can be viewed as springing from differences of interpretation, not of the original message, then the issue of their relationship with Islam should also be resolved.

Some might argue that the acceptance of Islam can be seen as an interpretation of Christ's call in the gospels, where the Parakletos, the Messiah, said, "And I will pray the Father, and he shall give you another Comforter, that he may abide with you for ever; Even the Spirit of truth; whom the world cannot receive because it seeth him not, neither knoweth him: but ye know him; for he dwelleth with you and shall be in you" (John 14:16–17). To this he added:

> If a man love me, he will keep my words, and my father will love him, and we will come unto him and make our abode with him. He that loveth me not, keepeth not my sayings: and the word which ye hear is not mine, but the Father's which sent me. These things have I spoken unto you, being yet present with you. But the Comforter which is the Holy Ghost, whom the Father shall send in my name, he shall teach you all things and bring all things to your remembrance, whatsoever I have said unto you. (John 14:23–26)
>
> When the Comforter is come, whom I will send unto you from the Father, even the Spirit of truth which proceedeth from the Father, he shall testify of me. And ye also shall bear witness, because ye have been with me from the beginning. (15:26–27)
>
> Nevertheless I tell you the truth; it is expedient for you that I go away: for if I go not away, the Comforter will not come unto you; but if I depart I will send him unto you. And when he is come he will reprove the world of sin, and of righteousness, and of judgment; Of sin, because they believe not on me; Of righteousness, because I go to my Father, and ye see me no more; Of judgment, because the prince of this world is judged. I have yet many things to say unto you yet you cannot bear them now. Howbeit, when he, the Spirit of truth is come, he will guide you into all truth: for he shall not speak of himself; but whatsoever he shall hear, that shall he speak: and he will show you things to come. He shall glorify me, for he shall receive of mine, and shall shew it unto you. All things that the Father hath are mine; therefore said I, that he shall take of mine and shall show it unto you. (16:7–15)

It could even be argued that for the medieval Bosnian Christians (*krstjani*), for whom the Gospel of Saint John was a key devotional text, this prophecy of Christ was fulfilled in the coming of Muhammad, as the greatest Defender or

Parakletos.[1] The acceptance of Islam by the Bosnian Christians may have resulted from their interpreting the Evangelist's message to mean that becoming Muslims would actually fulfill their faith and strengthen them in their waiting. This concept of the message of the Much Praised is found at the core of Islam, in its oldest interpretation.[2] Although the Koran questions the spread of interpretations of Christ and his gospel, it firmly bears witness to him and proclaims his message to be at the center of God's universal call, which is the same in essence although it takes numerous forms. This return to the original nature of Christ in order to overcome disagreement, division, and conflict is summed up in the statement: "The Messiah, Jesus son of Mary, was only the Messenger of God, and His Word that He committed to Mary, and a Spirit from Him. So believe in God and his Messengers and say not 'Three.' Refrain; better is it for you. God is only one God" (Koran 4:171).

Christ's mediation enables every individual in every age to approach God through his own individuality. This opportunity is proclaimed in Christ's words: "He that seeth me seeth him that sent me" (John 12:45). The self-same message was proclaimed by the prophet Muhammad.[3] This message ordains that all human individuals can have a mutual relationship with God. Whatever their time and place in the world of multiplicity and motion, they possess the potential to journey toward the stable Center. Christ and Muhammad's closeness to or shared identity with the Center means that every individual human movement toward transcendent unity demonstrates the presence of the supra-individual in the world of forms, the face of God in earthly appearances. Individual freedom expresses itself as an individual path. There are as many faiths as there are human individuals. The differences lie only in the symbols and languages through which the individuals unite themselves into communities or churches. Each of these communities, therefore, when it denies the universal nature of the Center and claims knowledge of and access to it as an exclusive possession, denies only itself.

1. Although this position is not undisputed, in the sum of facts known about the Bosnian Church it is generally agreed that the Bosnian Sufis are direct descendants of this church. Studies of contemporary man led the Sufis to this understanding of the name Parakletos, which is equivalent in meaning to that of Muhammad ("much praised"), and to the words "greatly good" in the Book of Genesis (1:31). See also Rusmir Mahmutćehajić, *Dobra Bosna* (Zagreb, 1997), 84, 113–15.

2. See *Life of Muhammad: A Translation of Ibn Ishaq's Sirat Rasul Allah,* with foreword, introduction, and notes, by A. Guillaume (Oxford, 1980), 104, a source outstanding for the light it sheds on the life of the Prophet: "*Menahhemana* (bless him and keep him) which is, in Syrian, *Muhammad;* and in Greek, *Paraclete.*"

3. This is quoted in several collections of the Prophet's teachings. According to *Sahih Muslim* (CMXLVIII, 5637), he said: "Who sees me sees the Truth."

The multitude of religious manifestations can return to unity only by way of their esoteric roots. Contemporary trends of thought, distinguished above all by a loss of sympathy for those esoteric elements of religion that have always assisted secular interpretations of God, humanity, and the universe, stress the differences between religious forms. These differences are interpreted as oppositions and ideologized as "conflict between civilizations." The culture of accepting differences and building harmonious relations between them is neither possible nor comprehensible at a level of simplistic totalitarian religious dogma. The absence of the lost Center is filled by contemporary theories about "conflicts between civilizations." This term is used to classify the conflicts between ethnic and religious communities, which the twentieth century has so often tried to solve with "divide and quit" theories (as in India, Cyprus, Northern Ireland, Bosnia-Herzegovina, and elsewhere). These conflicts and these attempts at their solution are a clear demonstration of humanity's inability to examine itself, and life as a whole, in order to identify the unity at the heart of the differences.

When the relationship between Islam, Catholicism, and Orthodoxy is observed from the viewpoint of local ethno-national ideology, which has developed mainly in the last two centuries, it is evident that universal religious elements have been seen as obstructing ethno-national identification. Religions have been given the role of supporting this ideology. Whenever a religion tried to bridge an alleged geopolitical division, it was criticized for naiveté or attacked for opposing "national needs." During the campaign to bind churches and religious organizations to political strategies, the principles of the holy teachings were either silenced or betrayed.

This produced tension, as the narrowing and hardening of national ideologies are hostile to religion's universal quality. Religious ethics were beaten down to the level of ethno-national strategies or ideological "isms" so that attacks on the Other were given an alleged basis in the religion itself. A mentality developed by which political organizations were seen as vitally connected with, or superior to, religious organizations. In this situation, the various Christian sects were aligned with European geopolitical trends on the basis of monetary, economic, and political union, while Islam was perceived as an un-European phenomenon.

This concept of Islam as anti-Western has been stressed ad nauseam, in fact—perhaps because politicized concepts of the world's religions are those that count. However, Islam, divided as it is from universality, is no more immune than Christianity to exploitation for ideological and social goals.

Contemporary relations between religious and political ideologies are also present in the interpretations of the Islamic element in the Bosnian drama. There are two principal views of Islam in Bosnia. The first places Islam in the framework of those readings of history that submit religion to the conflicts of political will in Europe. Islam is thus not only an active participant in these conflicts but also forms part of the anti-European coalition. The second, the vision of European development as vital for the world's future—that is, the advance of liberal democracy in the fullest sense of the word—is seen as confronted by the unacceptable anomaly of an Islam that is the tool of hostile political ideologies.

Perhaps this is the best place to answer a question that may have occurred to readers: why, in this essay, is there so much emphasis on the religious content of the Bosnian drama? In the current denial of Bosnia, which reached its destructive climax in the events of 1991–95, many of the factors in this drama remain fundamentally the same: that is, the old wine of Communist atheism has been poured into new, ostensibly "religious" bottles. Communist ideology is a structured denial of those human elements that find their expression in religion. It attempted to divide political and economic strategies from the essential contents of culture. Religion was reduced to a manipulative and oligarchic structure, and its universal quality reduced to "tribalism." It must be realized that an ideological interpretation founded on atheism is of primary importance for understanding the events and phenomena in Bosnia, which are indivisible from tradition, holy teaching, and religious wisdom. Therefore this essay is openly concerned with religious questions, although this may be incomprehensible to the many who feel that liberalism has driven out the need for religion. In fact, liberalism today is being transformed into a new "democratic" support for the same old Communist atheism.

The complexity of Bosnian society shows itself in manifold loyalties: toward religious and ethno-national communities and toward the unity of the state. In the Communist concept the first two loyalties were denied. Therefore, rebuilding Bosnia-Herzegovina into a genuine state is possible only with full emphasis on the need to reconcile all three loyalties. Political thinking, as an important factor in this rebuilding, should not include inherited interpretations of religion except with a full recognition and acknowledgment of the ways in which they have been abused. The confusion and conflict of today calls for the reordering of Bosnian-Herzegovinan society on the basis of mutual recognition and complete honesty, which is the only route to trust. Until this is achieved, universal rights will receive no acknowledgment or protection—by any side.

7

THE DENIAL OF BOSNIA

The development of the Croatian state as Catholic and the Serbian state as Orthodox is a natural consequence of Christian divisions within Europe. These states perceive themselves as heirs to the general European heritage, a heritage inseparable from Christianity that is now being transformed into a secular version known as "liberal democracy."

Since the Catholic and Orthodox religions are seen as closely connected to the political plan of establishing and developing a Croatian and a Serbian state, while the Muslims are excluded from any such link by dint of their "conversion," a Bosnian state has, according to the expansionist plans supported by this reading of Croatian and Serbian statehood, at least two defects. Its right to inherit the medieval Bosnian kingdom is blocked by the presence of the Muslims and their link with something other than post-Renaissance Europe. They cannot participate as equals, say the advocates of these plans, either in Christian ecumenical desires or in the journey toward a liberal-democratic Europe. They are therefore an obstacle that should be removed: a presence discordant with the political growth of Europe and one that interferes with the creation of "pure" Serbian-Croatian borders.

Every such view of their existence is based, above all, on a denial of the Bosniaks' right to be what they think they are. This denial is inevitably accompanied by an assertion of what they "really" are—that is, their role in the ideological plans of the Croatian and Serbian states. If they resist this categorization they are immediately accused of opposing "European values."

A precise statement of this model is given by Franjo Tuđman. The Bosniaks, according to him, "were for the most part, around 80 percent Croatian, but their religion subsequently divided them from the Croatian mainstream; most of them speak the *ikavski* dialect, which forms the connection between the Dalmatian and Slavonian Croats."[1]

This view has been expressed on numerous different occasions and in different ways. Its consequences for Bosnia-Herzegovina are explained (in a somewhat repetitious manner) by Petar Vučić:

> The Croatian state's integral strategy must be assured by the integration of all Croatian lands, so that this concept overlaps territorially with the concept of Croatia, and all Croatian lands are inside the Croatian state. Acknowledging Bosnia-Herzegovina as an independent state is against the interests of Croatia. Bosnia and Herzegovina are Croatian lands which should be integrated into Croatia. Croatia in its current borders should be understood as being merely the heartland, which in the course of time should be widened until the concepts of Croatia and of Croatian territory coincide both in concept and in fact.[2]

The dream of a Serbian ethno-national state bordering on this Croatian state has resulted in a second ethno-national strategy. In the last few centuries, both have constructed their own ethno-national hierarchies, ideologies, and infrastructures. Both strategies are characterized by a total denial of Bosnia-Herzegovina's historical, political, and cultural existence. This position is supported by the indecisiveness of the international community, as evident in the documents of the International Conference for the Former Yugoslavia held on 4 October 1992. These envisage the following five potential solutions to the Bosnia-Herzegovina drama, which by then had taken the form of war:

1. A centralized state.
2. A centralized federal state with significant functions devolved to between four and ten regions.
3. A loose federal state of three ethnic units which are not geographically connected.
4. A loose confederation of three ethnically organized republics with a po-

---

1. Conversation between D. Hudelist and F. Tuđman, *Globus,* 22 November 1996, 10.
2. P. Vučić, *Politička sudbina Hrvatske: geopolitičke, geostrateške karakteristike Hrvatske* [The political destiny of Croatia: Geopolitical and geostrategic characteristics of Croatia] (Zagreb, 1995), 419.

tentially significant degree of independence, including even matters of security.
5. A Muslim state, with Serbs owing allegiance to the Federal Republic of Yugoslavia, and Croats to Croatia.[3]

The acceptance of the potential destruction of Bosnia-Herzegovina evident in proposals 4 and 5 meant indirect international support for anti-Bosnianism. Bosnia-Herzegovina's unity was placed in question, fulfilling the chief demand of the warmongers.

It also tacitly acknowledged the motives for the commencement of war; that is, the claim that might is right. This was conveyed with a notable lack of ambiguity by Ratko Mladić: "The existence of the Republika Srpska may be contested internationally, but the existence of its army cannot be contested. The Republika Srpska exists because we have our territory, our nation, our government and all the attributes of a state. Whether they acknowledge it or not—that's their problem. The army is the fact." Mladić's speech then outlines a crude "historical theory about Bosnia-Herzegovina and the tensions between Serbia and Croatia."[4] Franjo Tuđman agreed: "This [the removal of the tensions] can be brought about so that the national goals of Serbia are achieved, and she has no more need for expansion; and simultaneously the borders of Croatia would be established, for her current pretzel-shape is unnatural." The disappearance of Bosnia-Herzegovina is, accordingly, the best solution both to the "Greater Serbian Question" and to Greater Croatia's effort to satisfy its own demands by meeting those of its ally: "It is in the Croatian interest to solve this problem in a natural way, in the same way as the Banovina problem was solved. Along with this there could remain a part, a 'statelet of Bosnia,' where Muslims would be a majority, and this Bosnian state could be a buffer zone between Croatia and Serbia. Thus the colonial artifact of Bosnia-Herzegovina would disappear," said Tuđman.[5]

Interpreting the Dayton Agreement in December 1995, Tuđman further explained why the division of Bosnia was the only rational solution, while blaming the formal recognition of Muslim national identity under Tito for aggravating problems between Croats and Serbs:

3. *International Conference on the Former Yugoslavia (ICFY), Working Paper on Constitutional Options,* 4 October 1992. This is a prepared draft offered to "the conflicting parties."
4. From D. Owen's *Balkan Odyssey* (London, 1996), 81–82.
5. Tuđman's replies to journalists, quoted in *Slobodna Dalmacija,* 31 December 1991–1 January 1992, 3–4.

Bosnia and Herzegovina, which, as a Turkish province, had been placed under the protectorate of Austria-Hungary by the decision of the Congress of Berlin, was established as a republic in the Yugoslav Federation. Although Bosnia and Herzegovina, owing to its position, was the central country of Yugoslavia, it could not act in any way as a stabilizing factor, since it was largely split between opposing civilizations. Communist fantasies that the growth of Croatian-Serbian national differences could be halted by proclaiming the population of Islamic faith to be a separate nation bore a fruit opposite to what had been hoped for.

Thus, by denying that the Bosniaks are a separate entity and by stressing their culpability for having "converted," the ground was prepared for resolving the tensions between Serbs and Croats—by dividing Bosnia. "Concerning this," Tuđman stated, "it is clear that the borders of Croatia, as they would become, would be stronger, so that no decision unacceptable to Croatian strategy could ever be passed." Here he refers to the Communist Party's internal decision, passed in 1968, to recognize the rights of Muslims to proclaim themselves as a separate entity, an option which had been denied them until then. According to Tuđman,

The division of Bosnia is the most important issue for Croatian-Serbian agreement—or even for a Croatian-Serbian war, if an agreement is not reached. Observe how all Serbian and Croatian thinking, on the eve of the Second World War, revolved around the concept of dividing Bosnia. This should be the way forward, to prevent a repetition of the horrors we have passed through before now.[6]

The flow of history is largely directed by selfish human needs to protect personal assets and achieve status; hence, economic development, as manifested in the democratic and free-market model of society, requires that the world as a whole submit to Western economic power and that the values on which it is founded be accepted. Anything that takes a shape different from these values should be denied on the basis of its discord with the nature and power of Christianity and liberal democracy. This is the agreed subtext of both Tuđman's and Kissinger's interpretation of Bosnian events. As Kissinger says:

I think that every national group in Bosnia should have the freedom to choose what it wants. This means that the defined part of Bosnia which

6. From *Oslobođenje,* 15 December 1995, 4.

wants to join Croatia should be given permission to do so. The same applies to the Bosnian Serbs and Serbia. I believe that there can, and should, be an independent Muslim state, but I would never insist that Croats and Serbs should live in such a state.[7]

This justification of the right to do as one desires incorporates the right to do whatever is within one's power. The total silence about the means by which these goals are to be accomplished can be interpreted as acknowledging the right to employ whatever means are at hand. Milošević and Tuđman both perceived this logic. They used all means at their disposal, and they did not trouble themselves with looking for a further green light. The Serbification and Croatization of Bosnia-Herzegovina territory required the annihilation of the Muslims by genocide in order to bring about the desired borders, so genocide was one of the methods used.

The readings of history outlined in this chapter deny all possibility that unity may be present in the world's diversity. They exclude all possibility that the Muslims may reach, by way of their own religion and culture, the center that the Serbs and Croats are aiming for. Muslims can only join this movement by "returning" to their allegedly Croatian or Serbian origins. This opens the way for the denial of all rights to Muslims in the community, while the Serbian and Croatian nationalist ruling elites are free to launch their campaign of "harmonizing" the inter-racial borders by all available means, even if this includes removing the Muslim presence by force. The only limit will be the limit of their own physical power.

7. Conversation between D. Butković and Henry Kissinger, *Globus,* 6 December 1996, 5–6.

8

The Bosnian-Herzegovinan model of unity in diversity is opposed to all ideologies that are based on exclusivity and ignore the call for charity toward others that is present in every religious teaching. But the latest war against the Bosnian paradigm has produced clear proof of how the promoters and supporters of these ideologies have rationalized and exploited their hatred. The events following one another thick and fast in the last few years are largely based on a logical matrix, although many episodes seem unrelated and unplanned at first sight. Many too remain hidden, as there has been considerable effort to hide the scope and savagery of the acts of destruction and killing.

Yugoslavia arose as a conglomeration of cultural, political, and historical entities. Some of its constituent parts were at least a thousand years older than the very idea of Yugoslavia. But Yugoslavia's original concept also included the desire that the individual entities of which this compound was formed should be assimilated and incorporated into the ideological design of a Greater Serbia.

This plan fueled concepts and acts contrary to the Yugoslav ideal. In particular, these manifested themselves in plans for homogenized states for Croats and Serbs: one state per nation, one incorporating all Serbs, the other all Croats. Since Bosnia's only contribution to this scheme could be the passive acceptance of its own destruction, it was excluded by its very nature from such a scheme. The fall of Yugoslavia and the rise of nation-state ideologies thus envisaged the fall of Bosnia. Parallel with the move toward "one state for all Serbs" (and one for all Croats), the demand for the deconstruction of Bosnia, to stop its interfering with the shape of "Serbian" or "Croatian" territory, was inevitable. This demand was treated with understanding, even sympathy, by most European observers and participants, who tended to disregard the medieval existence of the Bosnian Kingdom—for no apparent reason, except perhaps the religious changes under Turkish rule.

The demand that Croatian and Serbian territory should be "harmonized" developed, not surprisingly, into a campaign for the division of Bosnia as a precondition for resolving internal tensions. This was revealed most clearly during 1991, in the statements of the Serbian nationalist-socialist ruling elite as personified by Milošević. It was demanded that "Serbian autonomous regions" should be formed in Bosnian territory, which were accordingly (albeit illegally) established, and covered 63 percent of the total territory of Bosnia. This was followed by the demand of the Croatian nationalist elite, as personified by Tuđman, for "Croatian autonomous regions," covering 21 percent of Bosnia. These were proclaimed in the same manner as the "Serbian" regions, and an "autonomous Croatian government" was established over 21 percent of Bosnian state territory. (The overlap between the Serbian and Croatian autonomous areas covered 13 percent of the total territory).

Behind this division of Bosnian territory into "Serbian" and "Croatian" parts stood the notorious agreement between Milošević and Tuđman. But an overall view must include the contribution of certain international forces to the denial and division of the Bosnian state, both before the war and during the carving up of Bosnia. During the course of 1991, the international community accepted the positions at the heart of the Greater Serbian and Greater Croatian plans for Bosnia. The division of Bosnia-Herzegovina was established as the most important requirement for preventing possible conflict. Thus the international community aligned itself implicitly with the Serbian and Croatian ruling elites. The latter were thereby encouraged to reject everything that did not accord with the aims of their overall plan, while they accepted, ostensibly for the sake of peace, everything that supported their anti-Bosnian campaign. Bosnia was converted into three separate entities, while all links between them were severed.

Central to the original anti-Bosnian plan was "Serbian national unity" (including its Bosnian element) and "Croatian national unity" (again, including its Bosnian element). This duality had no place for the Muslims, who were virtually denied access to the arena of political action. They became a "separate entity," deprived of the powers of statehood. This was managed in such a way that they themselves became accessories to the plan to destroy Bosnia, if only by submitting to their "separate Bosnian entity." They were accorded only a strictly limited influence in political and military terms.

Radovan Karadžić and Mate Boban were simply those who carried out the will and plan of their superiors at the apex of the ethno-national pyramid. A division of spoils between the Serbian and Croatian ethno-national ruling elites was agreed upon, throwing the "responsibility" for preventing a peaceful outcome on the Muslims. Thus, at the beginning of 1992 Karadžić complained of difficulties in "defining national territories with the Muslim side." This carve-up, agreed upon between the two ethno-nationalist camps, underlay every approach, every offer of cooperation, every discussion on restructuring Bosnia. Meanwhile, the Bosniaks found themselves defined more and more as the "third side" that was stubbornly and criminally resisting a peaceful solution.

Thus the situation was presented as one of tension between three ethno-national plans, each of which corresponded to a certain ethno-national elite, ideology, and organization. The conflict between them was purported to be the natural consequence of implacable hatreds, differences of culture, and similar causes. Meanwhile, their leaders awaited the response of the international community, expecting this to take the form of "divide and quit." This expectation was largely fulfilled in the international approach to the war against Bosnia-Herzegovina. From the beginning of 1992, all peace talks accepted the premise of territorial division as the most effective way of stopping the war and reconciling the "inter-ethnic" differences.

This may explain why David Owen, at the very beginning of his Bosnian mission, was so ready to claim that there were in principle no differences between the conflicting sides. "Within a week after taking the position of Co-chairman [of the negotiations], I had come to realize, and to say publicly, that there were no innocents among the political and military leaders in all three parties in Bosnia-Herzegovina."[1]

The result was an acceptance of the results of genocide in all subsequent negotiations, so that the gradual emasculation or defeat of the Muslim side was viewed as providing the best way out. Here we should remember the original arms embargo, which, at the request of Milošević, was passed at the end of 1991 by the U.N. Security Council. The ultimate effect of this decision was to prevent the Bosniaks from defending themselves from attack by their neighbors. The forces sponsored by Milošević had enough weapons and ammunition for a decade of war, and those of Tuđman were able to obtain them in

1. Owen, *Balkan Odyssey,* 47.

unlimited quantities due to the nature of Croatia's frontiers. Therefore, the proclamation of the Muslims' "military defeat" in a string of crucial peace talks was in express accordance with the wishes of the instigators and agents of the strategy of division by force.

The original plan of carving up Bosnia-Herzegovina into "Serbian" and "Croatian" regions was encouraged by suggestions for "ethno-national" cantons, provinces, units, regions, states, republics, and so on. All peace proposals—initially known by the names of their chief creators (the Cutileiro, Vance-Owen, and Owen-Stoltenberg plans, as well as the Washington Agreement, the Contact Group Plan, and the Dayton Agreement)—accepted a false concept of Bosnia by accepting its division on an ethno-national basis. This, of course, was always more or less in harmony with the aggressors' plans for building an enlarged Serbia and an enlarged Croatia on the remains of the ancient European country of Bosnia-Herzegovina.

Thus the peace talks, however the international participants may have viewed them, were understood by the destroyers as both an excuse and an invitation to continue implementing genocide by all means available. For if the international community acknowledged by its approach that interethnic hostility was the fundamental cause of the current and future disintegration of the Bosnian state—which was the aggressors' line—then segregation could be presented as necessary and desirable.[2] Therefore, as the genocidal division of Bosnia-Herzegovina proceeded, it only increased the determination of the international community to resolve the situation by "separating the peoples."

Initially, the favored idea was to have a large number of provinces, structured primarily on the basis of ethnic principles to the point of virtually comprising a union of three ethnic states. This would lead naturally toward the

---

2. The war against Bosnia and Herzegovina was initiated with the full cruelty of killing and destruction and persecution by the end of 1991. It was the culmination of the dissolution of Yugoslavia. All controversies and tensions of Yugoslavia's composition were manifested within the war. Many reviews and interpretations have already been offered on the history and participants and constellations of different participants within it. A systematic and summarized review of its causes and effects has been given in Ivo Banac, "Post-Yugoslav Realities: State and Ethnicity," which was read on 4 June 1998, at the international conference "Unfinished Peace," Zagreb. The significance of this interpretation lies in its foundation on integral insight into the nature of ethno-national identities and tensions among them. Predominantly, they were covered by the ideological mantel of the Yugoslav communist system. Further significant considerations on the same issue can be found in Ivo Banac, *The National Question in Yugoslavia: Origins, History, Politics* (Cornell, 1984). The cause and effect relationship of the destruction of Bosnia and Herzegovina in its constitutional situation has been systematically covered in Edin Šarčević, *Ustav i p tika: Kritika etničkih ustava i postrepubličkog ustavotvorstva u Bosni i Hercegovini* [The constitution and politics: A critical review of ethnic constitutions and post-republic constitutionality in Bosnia and Herzegovina] (Sarajevo, 1997).

two-way division of Bosnia, with one part becoming a "national Serbian state," and the other, according to Tuđman, a territory entrusted to Croatia by the international community as a protectorate with the aim of "Europeanizing" the Muslims.[3]

3. On 29 May 1994, Tuđman announced to the editors of various newspapers that the Federation of Bosnia and Herzegovina had been set up by agreement of the United States, Europe, and Canada (here he was probably referring to the Washington Agreement) as a Croatian protectorate.

9

The fall of Yugoslavia demonstrated that some constitutional values were tending to weaken and disappear, while others were growing bigger and stronger. The plans of the nationalists came up against the existing state borders as an obstacle to their imperialist campaign. Therefore ethno-national unity and state borders became the most important elements of political thought. Those who were bent on transforming the Yugoslav region, on the basis of demands for "one nation, one state," demanded that the existing borders be changed. But those who demanded that the borders remain unaltered were forced, as the constituent republics became independent, to understand that in such circumstances the internal organization of the new states had to be established on principles other than those which had been promoted under the Yugoslav model.

This applied particularly to Bosnia. Its defense and survival as a unified state depended on the principle of unchanging borders, but also on the need for the peoples within Bosnia to put their relationships on a different footing. Any solution that did not endanger Bosnia's state unity should have been acceptable. This in turn would have required meeting any request of the Bosnian Serbs and Croats as long as it was compatible with the survival of Bosnia as a state. This type of policy should have sought support exclusively within a framework of European legal thought and European values. It should have been inspired, activated, and developed by a European framework, while simultaneously making whatever deals necessary to ensure its survival.

The possibility of such a strategy for Bosnia-Herzegovina was feared by those intent on destroying the Bosnian state and setting up lasting international borders between the Serbs and the Croats. Thus the Greater-State puppetmasters agreed that matters that divided them should be swiftly settled, making the conflict between Serbs and Croats marginal and the conflict with the Muslims central. This is shown in the statement of Ivan Aralica: "Not the Serbs—our problem with them is over. The Muslims have become the main problem in our neighborhood, we're keeping a close eye on them."[1] It is possible to quote numerous variations on this statement in the service of the Greater Serbian cause, with "Serbs" substituted for "Croats."

Forcing the unity of Bosnia-Herzegovina into the mold of opposition between Croats and Serbs on the one hand and Muslims on the other had the psychological effect of deflecting European attention away from the elites, ideologies, and organizations that were carrying out genocide against the Bosniaks. European public opinion began to see Bosnia less as a bridge between different religions and more as a Trojan horse that might bring the threat of "Islamic fundamentalism" into the West. This impression was reinforced by the political tensions between Bosniaks who formed a welter of conflicting ethnonational ideologies, political parties, religious communities, humanitarian organizations, and so on.

Pseudo-messianic leadership merely muddied the waters, enabling the supporters of the division of Bosnia to justify loudly and successfully their fight against this country. The waverings of Bosniak politics and its inconsistent approach to the religious chaos aroused the concern even of those who knew about the mass genocidal killings of Bosniaks and felt obliged to protect the state of Bosnia. Although it was of vital importance to avoid arousing anti-Muslim prejudice, Bosniak policy was betrayed on many occasions into acts that were most likely to provoke such prejudice. This cannot be explained without taking into account the fact that direct and indirect enemies of Bosnian statehood were active within Bosniak politics.

In Bosnia there were many areas where Bosniaks, Croats, or Serbs were in the majority, and many more places where they formed minorities. Thus the possibility of dividing Bosnia, considering the complexity of such an undertaking, could be contemplated only if the changes were made by means acceptable to the Western world. Tolerating any other approach meant express or implicit support for genocide.

The question of Bosniak survival, in fact, must be viewed in the context of

1. I. Aralica, *Šta sam rekao o Bosni* [What I said about Bosnia] (Zagreb, 1995), 84.

the geopolitical transformation of Europe. This means accepting at least two premises regarding the future: first, that non-European theories of state and law are unacceptable in the European geopolitical space; and, second, that integrationist movements in Europe are crucially dependent on the military, political, and economic stance of the United States of America. Every political act that ignores these premises spells doom for its supporters and implementors. Hence it was a simple matter for the Greater Serbian and Greater Croatian forces to accuse the Bosniaks of anti-European intentions while encouraging and supporting those elements in Bosniak politics that did not understand the principles of political action in today's Europe. This skillful policy of simultaneous support, incrimination, and division can be traced throughout the establishment and implementation of the anti-Bosnian matrix. While one cannot prove that the many ex-Communist Party apparatchiks who took up key positions in the Bosnia-Herzegovina state were carrying out the wishes of their former masters, their blinkered thought patterns were a ready source of support for the anti-Bosnian strategy.[2]

To understand the course of the destruction of Bosnia it is of vital importance to note the relationship between current European political trends and the recent wish to do away with the separation of church and state. The anti-Bosnian forces strove to use the "Islamic element" in Bosnian state politics as the key pretext for putting "Muslimhood" at the center of the Bosnia-Herzegovinan question, thus enabling them to present the partition of Bosnia as a marginal, secondary phenomenon. Great service was rendered to the anti-Bosnian forces by some former members of the Communist Party who aligned themselves with Alija Izetbegović, praising, without any sense of proportion or good taste, his "messianic role" and his "act of salvation."

The Bosnian state having been thus reduced to "the Muslim faction," the destroyers of the Bosnian state now had seemingly irrefutable arguments on their side. As for those Bosniak political forces that, in the context of the Bosnian state, based their demands only on the principle of equal and incontestable rights for all, Izetbegović's *Islamic Declaration* robbed them of legitimacy:

> The first and foremost conclusion is always the incompatibility of Islam and non-Islamic systems. There can be neither peace nor co-existence between the Islamic faith and non-Islamic social and political institutions. . . .

2. It is possible to list the names of a large number of former Communist Party members still employed in key positions in the state of Bosnia-Herzegovina. See, e.g., M. Alibabić, *Bosna u kandžama KOS-a* [Bosnia in the claws of the KOS] (Sarajevo, 1996); additional evidence can be found in Sefer Halilović, *Lukava strategija* [Cunning strategy] (Sarajevo, 1997).

In its assertion of the right to organize its own world, Islam clearly excluded any foreign ideology on its territory from the right or possibility of action. There is, moreover, no such thing as "the secular principle," and the state should be the expression of and support for the moral precepts of religion.[3]

When this statement of Izetbegović's is cited in the political arena, Bosniak policy—reasonably enough—cannot but appear to be a danger threatening all. But since this vision of Islam conveniently fits the European stereotype, it is clear that the final losers must ultimately be the Bosniaks. For Bosnia cannot survive unless it agrees on how its existence should be defended and unless it realizes that its acceptance in both a local and a wider European context is vital.

3. Alija Izetbegović, *Islamska deklaracija* [Islamic declaration] (Sarajevo, 1990), 98.

It is important to stress the nature of this controversial work. Its nucleus evolved at the end of the 1960s, in a circle of fervent Muslim opponents of communist totalitarianism. Claiming to oppose ideological rigidity, they attempted to formulate a so-called Islamic ideological antithesis to the communist synthesis that they despised. The final credit for the work went to Alija Izetbegović, one of its authorsnone of whom actually intended, or were capable of, applying the work to the world they lived in.

Persecuted in the real world, they turned to abstractions: an all-embracing solution, a distant salvation, a messianic dream. Ironically, the text was tailor-made for the authors of Bosnia's destruction: they saw it as key evidence for their allegations of the Muslim peril, using it to justify their murderous onslaught on Bosnia and Herzegovina. Moreover, of those who knew nothing of the true nature of tradition, many latched on to this work with religious fervor: members of the collapsing communist government for whom ideology was only skin-deep; disappointed and fearful members of the disintegrating totalitarian system and of the toppling structures of party, police, and the military; holders of privilege in financial organizations and state enterprises; those with "connections" in the state security apparatus, and so on. None had even an elementary knowledge of religion: for them the work offered an easy interpretation of their changing world, a means of ingratiating themselves with the new rulers, and a fresh justification for their fight to retain their privileges. This gave the work an unexpectedly wide readership, as the the destruction of Bosnia and Herzegovina continued apace. The position of power its author came to hold, and the general state of mental confusion and terror, gave the work additional impact.

10

A "MUSLIM STATE"

The plan for destroying Bosnia was founded, according to this thesis, on a historical construct that denied the historical existence of any Bosnian entity, political or cultural. It was accompanied by a campaign aimed at convincing a regional and international public that the Serbian and Croatian ethno-national plans were in fact the only legitimate forces of cohesion in Bosnia. These plans, presented as two unbroken Christian traditions, were allegedly kept from successful implementation only by the historical anomaly of "mass conversion to Islam." This was the main obstacle to forming "brotherly borders" and the consequent establishment of cordial Serbian-Croatian relations. As Mate Boban put it: "The Serbs are our brothers in Christ, but the Muslims are nothing to us, apart from the fact that for hundreds of years they raped our mothers and sisters."[1]

Radovan Karadžić has this contribution to make: "Serbs and Croats were never enemies before 1918, when they entered a joint state. Serbs and Croats will never be enemies again, once they separate their states." He also maintains that "Serbs cannot live together with Muslims and Croats."[2]

These statements, as publicly attested evidence shows, are deliberate steps toward the systematic "development" and "harmonization" of relations be-

1. Quotation ascribed to M. Jergović, *Tjednik,* 11 July 1997 (Zagreb), 7.
2. Quoted in Owen, *Balkan Odyssey,* 200.

tween one, two, three, or more ethno-national elites, ideologies, and pressure groups.

The dream of identifying and separating two ethnic states with boundaries passing through Bosnia, thus splitting it into two portions, "Croatian" and "Serbian," threatened to separate the Serbian and Croatian components from the population as a whole. The state would be reduced to just its Bosniak element. Any Bosniak claims to be defending Bosnia-Herzegovina could then be dismissed as a smoke screen concealing an equally nationalist project of territorial annexation. This would justify division, as the Serbs and Croats could then claim the same rights as the Bosniaks to annex territory. Formal division would be the logical next step, and international forces would no longer be able to object, as a recognizable unified state would no longer exist.

This scheme is evident in a series of events starting from the beginning of 1991. The private agreement between Franjo Tuđman and Slobodan Milošević, signed on 25 March in Karađorđevo, "honoring the interests of the Serbian and Croatian nations in full," points to the clear intention of dividing Bosnia-Herzegovina. Its parts were to be annexed to Serbia and Croatia, whose boundaries were to be redrawn. The behind-the-scenes nature of this deal meant that Milošević did not publicly mention the details of the agreed strategy. But his actions speak for themselves: they agree perfectly with the strategy adopted and supported by the rest of the Serbian ethno-national hierarchy. Its ideology is given its most frequent expression by Dobrica Ćosić, who, speaking of the "so-called constitutional peoples" of Bosnia-Herzegovina, states that they "cannot and will not live together any longer."[3] Proclaiming life together to be impossible is a precondition for justifying a Greater Serbia. If the claimed impossibility is not yet a fact, the next step is to make it so.

The role and significance of Milošević is defined by Ćosić in state-building terms: "Slobodan Milošević, who does not stand for nationalism as an ideology, but for statehood as a national goal, became a politician for his people, and a leader because of his charisma."[4]

Franjo Tuđman, unlike his Serbian counterpart, did reveal some of the contents of the Karađorđevo agreement on various occasions and in various ways.[5] The ideological, military, and organizational connection of the Bosnian

3. D. Ćosić, speaking with a Greek parliamentary delegation, 11 March 1993; quoted in *Borba,* 12 March 1993 (Belgrade), 3.

4. D. Ćosić, *Promene* [Changes] (Novi Sad, 1992), 141.

5. Owing to the anti-Muslim component at the heart of Greater Serb ideology, Milošević and Tuđman, in their plan for the division of Bosnia, included right from the beginning the necessity of destroying all trust and confidence between Croats and Bosniaks, which had been established and developed over a long period of joint opposition to Greater Serb designs. This trust had developed into a general political agreement, which many Bosniak intellectuals understood as "national unity." The cam-

Serbs with the ethno-national oligarchy of "the united Serbian nation," and of the Bosnian Croats with the equivalent ruling elite of "all the Croats," lay behind this agreement to "honor the interests of the Serbian and Croatian peoples in full." These interests would be met by dividing Bosnia-Herzegovina. If the state could be reduced to Muslims only, its collapse would be inevitable. Collapse would then become formal division.

Therefore, if Muslims were to demand that Bosnia-Herzegovina be reformed to meet the requirements of their own ethno-national ideology and ruling hierarchy, they would be providing the best possible support for Milošević and Tuđman's intentions to "honor the interests of the Serbian and Croatian nations in full"—that is, as these interests were defined by the two nationalist leaders. It is possible, therefore, to argue that the phenomenon best described as a "Muslim state" was envisioned from the start as a crucial component of the anti-Bosnian plan. "The major issue regarding a peaceful solution," remarked Tuđman in the early summer of 1991, "is that of demarcating the borders between Croatia and Serbia and of resolving the Muslim problem here." He agreed that this could be achieved by establishing a "Muslim state."[6]

According to the testimony of Warren Zimmermann, Tuđman claimed that Bosnia should be divided between the Croats and the Serbs. "Tuđman admitted that he had discussed these fantasies with Milošević, the Yugoslav Army leadership, and the Bosnian Serbs," writes Zimmermann, "and they agreed that the only solution is to divide up Bosnia between Serbia and Croatia."

Magnanimously, Tuđman declared he did not insist on a fifty-fifty division:

> Let Milošević take the larger half; he controls it anyway. We can make do with less than fifty percent. We're willing to leave the Muslims a small area around Sarajevo. They may not like it, but a stable Balkans is possible only if there's a change in Bosnia's borders, no matter what the Muslims think.

---

paign of Tuđman to divide Bosnia, following his agreement with Milošević, was accompanied by measures to destroy this confidence. This revealed his dedication to and deep involvement in the anti-Bosnian conspiracy. It also to explains the order for the "total cleansing" of Stolac, one of the key symbols of Bosniak culture. Stolac was outside the arena of military conflict, and the destruction of its "non-Croat" heritage represents one of the greatest crimes of the recent war. There is, however, another interpretation to explain the widespread destruction of this city. Tuđman, according to a source close to the Croatian president, saw Stolac as one of the most important strategic points for the defense of the planned Croatian Territory, if the area from Neum to Prevlaka, including Dubrovnik, had to be ceded to the Serbs. A third possibility is that this crime was committed on the basis that the Bosniaks had to be kept from coastal cess, in Tuđman's view, by a cordon sanitaire of at least 100 kilometers.

6. Quoted in T. Judah, "Belgrade Ready for Border Sacrifices to Preserve Unity," *The Times* (London), 13 May 1991.

There's nothing sacred about those borders. Bosnia isn't an ancient state like Croatia, which once extended all the way to Zemun.[7]

In a conversation between Tuđman, Milošević, and Izetbegović in Split on 28 March 1991, Tuđman told Izetbegović that Bosnia within its current borders was not viable as a state, so division would be necessary. To support his theory, Tuđman argued the impossibility of establishing a Bosnian government in Eastern Herzegovina, as the Serbs already held sway there, and hinted at the unlikelihood of Croatian cooperation with the Bosnian Government in Western Herzegovina.

Defined and interpreted in such terms, the ultimate status to be allocated to these regions became clear in Tuđman's next argument: that they are in reality a natural extension of the ethno-national territory of Serbs and Croats and have no actual ties to the Bosnian-Herzegovinan state. By way of conclusion, Tuđman suggested that the Muslims should establish "their" national state in central Bosnia, the "Bosnian statelet" described by the tenth-century chronicler Porphyrogenitus. This, according to Tuđman, would be the only way in which the Muslims could finally resolve their "national question."[8]

While making concerted efforts to urge Muslims toward acceptance of the "Muslim state" policy, according to Mario Nobilo, Milošević and Tuđman discussed in at least two meetings how to dismantle Bosnia-Herzegovina. He claims that they both fully agreed that the key issue was the creation of a Muslim state in central Bosnia and a voluntary exchange of territory. According to Nobilo, Tuđman said, "If the Muslims believe they can turn the whole of Bosnia-Herzegovina into an Islamic state, they are wrong. There should be some deal. If they want a sovereign state we would respect it. It would be the size of Slovenia—they should seriously consider it."[9]

7. W. Zimmermann, *Origins of a Catastrophe: Yugoslavia and Its Destroyers* (New York, 1996), 182.

8. The quoted facts of this dialogue were given to the writer immediately upon Izetbegović's arrival in Sarajevo. Tuđman expressed this concept on several occasions in various wordings. On one occasion he proclaimed: "This [reconciliation of Serb-Croat tensions] can be accomplished so that the national goals of Serbia are realized and she no longer has any motive for expansion, and consequently Croatia would be able to include her border-lands, for her current pretzel-shape is unnatural." Or, "It is in Croatia's interests to solve this problem in a straightforward way, the way in which the Banovine were formed. In addition a little 'mini-state' of Bosnia, could remain, where Muslims would be in the majority, and this Bosnian state could be a buffer zone between Croatia and Serbia. Thus the colonial creation of Bosnia and Herzegovina would disappear" (from Tuđman's New Year press conferences, *Slobodna Dalmacija,* 31 December 1991 and 1 January 1992).

9. This information can be found in an article by T. Judah, "Creation of Islamic Buffer State Discussed in Secret," *The Times* (London), 12 July 1991: "A senior advisor to Franjo Tuđman, the Croatian President, confirmed yesterday that secret talks have taken place between the leaders of Serbia and Croa-

At the end of 1991, Radovan Karadžić, with Momčilo Krajišnik, Aleksa Buha, Nikola Koljević, and Biljana Plavšić, presented Alija Izetbegović with a serious proposal that the Muslims should establish their own state in part of Bosnia. As far as the Serbs were concerned, the Muslims could, if they wished, run this state on "Islamic" principles.[10] It was obvious that this proposal was made with the full consent of Milošević and Tuđman, both now willing to hold out the bait of a "Muslim state" as the means to their own end. Once the principle of destroying the state of Bosnia and Herzegovina was accepted, it would be a simple matter to carve up its remains as and when the two powers desired.

This scheme was cynical and criminal—but also paradoxical. Cynical because it established the perfect motive for the other two nations to accuse and attack the nation in whose name the plan was allegedly conceived. Criminal because it could not be implemented without division and genocide. Paradoxical because it actually exploited what it accused the Muslims of doing— scheming to build an "Islamic state." (It is highly probable, in other words, that the anti-Bosnian ruling elites secretly supported, encouraged, and even financed what they publicly attacked: the direct and indirect campaigning by advocates of a "Muslim state.")

"The Muslims," Tuđman explained to Zimmermann,

> want to establish an Islamic fundamentalist state. They plan to do this by flooding Bosnia with 500,000 Turks. Izetbegović has also launched a demographic threat. He has a secret policy to reward large families so that in a few years the Muslims will be a majority in Bosnia. The influence of an Islamic Bosnia will then spread through Sandžak and Kosovo to Turkey and to Libya. Izetbegović is just a fundamentalist front man for Turkey: together they're conspiring to create a Greater Bosnia. I tell you, Mr. Ambassador, that if we in Croatia abandon the Croats in Bosnia to such a fate, they will turn on us. Some will become terrorists, and they won't spare Zagreb in their acts of revenge.[11]

In the consensus that Tuđman and Milošević allegedly reached at Karađorđevo to "protect the interests of the Serbian and Croatian nations in full," the twin goals were a "Greater Croatia" as a state for all Croats and a

---

tia to resolve the Yugoslav conflict by carving up the republic of Bosnia-Herzegovina and creating an Islamic buffer-state between them. 'It's on the table,' said Mario Nobilo. 'Maybe this is now the best option for a lasting solution.' " In the same article it is later added, "Mr. Nobilo said that Dr. Tuđman and Slobodan Milošević, the Serb leader, had discussed the deal in at least two meetings."

10. The writer took part in the negotiations during which Radovan Karadžić issued this statement.

11. Zimmermann, *Origins of a Catastrophe,* 181–82.

"Greater Serbia" as a state for all Serbs. This was the subject of a secret document signed by a group of twenty-two Bosnian Croats on 12 November 1991. The document is unequivocal: "The Croatian people in Bosnia-Herzegovina must finally undertake a decisive and active policy which will lead to the realization of our ancient dream—a united Croatian state."[12]

Denying Bosnia-Herzegovina's right to existence, urging Muslims to resolve their "national question" by means of a "Muslim state," and warning of "the Muslim threat" to both Catholics and Orthodox served as a smoke screen and a pretext for a pre-set goal. The Muslim State scheme was an essential part of the plan for disabling and destroying Bosnia-Herzegovina and should have been internationally recognized as such.

The first purpose of the scheme was to create the impression that the Muslims themselves could be persuaded to accept such a plan. During the course of later events, there were many explicit efforts to drive Muslim policy in this direction.[13] It is publicly known that agreements and plans for the destruction of Bosnia-Herzegovina were in existence well before the beginning of the war in spring 1992. The Republic of Croatia was recognized as an independent state in December 1992, and more than three months passed before the recognition of Bosnia-Herzegovina. During this time, the plans continued to unfold within the Croatian leadership. They were aware that Bosnian independence would buy time by preventing the complete establishment of a puppet Serbian regime in the country. Meanwhile, during the probable Serbian attack on the newly independent Bosnia, the plan to carve up territory between Croats and Serbs could take effect.

These plans and agreements bore fruit in the establishment of new politico-military organizations. Those set up ostensibly on behalf of Bosnian Croats were totally committed to the will of the ethno-national elite in Zagreb. Those created for the Bosnian Serbs were far more formidable, as they consisted of sizable elements from the military and political hierarchies of former Yugoslavia, as well as being totally committed to the Belgrade ethno-national

---

12. *Bosnia Report* (London), November-December 1997, 9. This document was published on 13 October 1997, in *Feral Tribune* (Split). It was signed by Mate Boban, Vladimir Šoljić, Božo Raić, Ivan Bender, Petar Marković, Dario Kordić, and others. As is clear from the document itself, it was based on the conclusions of the meetings held on 13 and 20 June 1991, between its signatories and Tuđman.

13. At the end of 1992, Poljak, a colonel in the Croatian army, promised the top-ranking members of the Bosnia-Herzegovina Army every kind of military help on condition that they established a "Muslim Army." This promise, regularly accompanied by threats, could be heard from most Croat officials who met at that time with representatives of the Bosnian-Herzegovinan Army. Documented cases include the testimony concerning N. Obradović and I. Andabak, officers of the Croatian Army (HV) and the Croatian Defense Council (HVO).

elite. Moreover, the role played by the state media in this process is well-documented.

Its declaration of independence left Bosnia-Herzegovina divided between the influence and actions of Serbia and Croatia, in accordance with their agreement for the carve-up of Bosnia. Influence and management from Belgrade and Zagreb was implemented through two entities: the Republika Srpska and its later counterpart the Croatian Community of Herceg-Bosna (initially, the Republic of Herceg-Bosna).

Both organizations are politically and militarily opposed to the state of Bosnia-Herzegovina. They deny its existence as a state, presenting it as a "Muslim usurpation." Limited only by their military capacity, they have eradicated all traces of Bosnia-Herzegovina's multiconfessional structure and have established ethno-national homogeneity throughout all the territory in their power by means of expulsions and killings.

In their campaign against Bosnian-Herzegovinan unity, the de facto leaders, that is, the Zagreb and Belgrade ruling elites, counted on the international community's acquiescence to the theory of "divide and quit." The world powers were known to want peace at the lowest possible price and level of involvement. All that was required was a judicious information campaign. The forces defending Bosnia-Herzegovina were reduced to "the Muslim faction" in order to rob them of all legitimacy in their struggle for sovereignty and international recognition. The anti-Bosnian conspiracy now only awaited confirmation of the Bosniaks' acceptance of this criminal matrix and the eventual inclusion of official Bosniak policy within it.

From the testimony of David Owen and his manner of approach, it can be concluded that he saw no difference in principle between the "sides": all wanted "nation states" and were only fighting over the amount of territory that would belong to each.[14] All peace proposals, therefore, started from the premise that a clear definition of three ethno-national territories was necessary to stop the war.[15] This meant accepting as a starting-point the demands of Milošević and Tuđman that Bosnia be disestablished as a multi-ethnic state.

However, the Bosniak political tradition contained little or nothing that could be used to support division or even make it remotely attractive. Though the Bosniak participants in the negotiations did not offer satisfactory resistance

14. See, for example, Owen, *Balkan Odyssey,* 207, 218.

15. These proposals became known as the Carrington-Cutileiro Plan, the Vance-Owen Peace Plan (VOPP), the *Invincible* Peace Package (the Owen-Stoltenberg plan of establishing a union of three republics), the European Union Action Plan (EUAP), and the Contact Group Initiative (CGI). These were the basis for the plans produced in 1994 and 1995.

to these plans for division, fierce resistance was encountered in Bosnia-Herzegovina itself. The resulting forced compromise, aimed at achieving a "sustainable peace" by the establishment of a "Muslim Republic," was explained by David Owen as follows: "The European Union was never opposed to a separate Muslim state, if that came about by popular consent." [16]

The leading Bosniak politicians worked hard to drum up consent to this "Muslim Republic," even though Bosnia-Herzegovina's forces of resistance were gradually organizing themselves and gathering strength. This enabled David Owen, chief representative of the European Union in the peace talks and a subsequent advocate of the "divide and quit" policy, to maintain (in August 1993) that "Izetbegović was now moving toward a separate Muslim republic, and that realistic talk of keeping Bosnia-Herzegovina together was over." [17]

Thus the main aim became one of slowly but surely reducing the Bosnian state to "the Muslim faction," paving the way for the Bosniak political leadership to request that Bosnia be reconstituted as a union of three states, one of them "Muslim." Virtually all actions of the Bosniak political leaders, starting as early as summer 1993, were geared toward this end. The principle of division had been accepted, and further talks focused on percentages and details.

The Bosnian-Herzegovinan public, overwhelmed by destruction and slaughter, knew very little of what the negotiations were actually about. Exploiting this fact, the supporters of division made every attempt to get decisions passed that would enable a three-way dismantling of Bosnia-Herzegovina. Between September and November 1993, the doers of this dirty work became convinced that Bosnia would be transformed into three ethnonational states. The Muslim state would incorporate 33.5 percent of Bosnian territory; the Bosnian Serbs would take 49 percent of the territory; and the Bosnian Croats would be apportioned 17.5 percent of the territory. [18]

Acceptance of division by the political elite is confirmed by the fragmentary statements fed to the Bosnian-Herzegovinan public. Alija Izetbegović mentioned it explicitly for the first time in November 1993, in Zenica. This was fol-

16. Owen, *Balkan Odyssey*, 273.

17. Ibid., 224.

18. David Owen testifies on this issue: "Shortly before Tuđman had to leave for Brussels, a joint agreement was reached on a map claimed to provide over 33.3 percent for the Muslim republic. We checked the exact figures by computer that evening, and found the total was 33.5 percent. The Serbs an the Croats had agreed to leave aside their own boundaries, for example in Posavina and above Dubrovnik, for further discussion, but the Serbs committed themselves to finding 17.5 percent for the majority Croatian republic. This was the moment when the 49 percent/51 percent division of Bosnia Herzegovina between the Serbs on the one hand and the Croats and Muslims on the other came about, the result of months of hectare-by-hectare negotiations" (ibid., 256).

lowed by his better-known announcement of 27 August, in a speech delivered to the first wartime parliament of Bosnia-Herzegovina: "It appears that we must divide. We can do this at the negotiating table, or on the battlefield in war, where, sadly, all laws are gradually losing their force."

Soon, in various discussions, many around him started to support the idea. It should not be forgotten that systematic pressure was being exerted on the Bosniak leadership and intellectuals to "change their goals," a pressure intensified by siege conditions, bombardments, mass murder, destruction, and terror. (This pressure was inflicted, for the most part, by erstwhile members of Yugoslavia's key military and political echelons and in the Belgrade power centers where the destruction of Bosnia-Herzegovina was designed and managed.)[19]

The results of this pressure became visible to all when the Bosniak Congress was held in Sarajevo on 27 September 1993. The delegates were prepared for the meeting by handouts explaining the Owen-Stoltenberg proposal for establishing three ethno-national states in Bosnia-Herzegovina, a suggestion that agreed at all points with the original positions of Milošević and Tuđman. When, after a discussion lasting for several hours, it became obvious that the "Muslim state" would be rejected, a specially formulated demand was submitted to the delegates for approval. The demand implicitly accepted the concept of a Muslim state, with the precondition that all "territory occupied by force" be returned.[20] Thus the concept of Bosnia-Herzegovina's unity was denied, and the extent of the Muslim State's territory was prioritized as the central issue of the Bosnian drama.

Thus the anti-Bosnian concept of a "Bosnian Republic," as envisaged by Milošević and Tuđman, who saw it as central to their anti-Bosnian strategy, was accepted. In line with preparations for the acceptance of this proposal, the reduction of the constitution and state organizations of Bosnia-Herzegovina to their "Muslim" equivalents commenced. This process was most systematically carried out within the Army of the Republic of Bosnia-Herzegovina, which—with the warmest Croatian encouragement—was transformed into a "Muslim" army (see footnotes).

---

19. In the summer of 1993, F. Muslimović, former chief of the KOS for Bosnia and Herzegovina, convinced the participants at a session of the Council of Muslim (now Bosniak) Intellectuals that "a change of goals" was necessary. This would mean that the Muslims would now fight only for territories where they had been in the majority before the war. Here he was merely interpreting the position of the Bosnia political leader.

20. Report on the voting of the participants in the "Bosniak Congress," *Oslobođenje,* 29 September 1993, 2.

For additional evidence of support for a "third state," one need go no further than the public statements of Enes Duraković and Adnan Jahić.[21] Jahić, accepting a leading role among the supporters of the plan, while it was still at the margins of Bosniak politics, went beyond his brief by writing the following:

> The territory which remains under the control of our Bosnian-Herzegovinan army will be a Muslim state; the Muslim state will be the national state of the Bosniaks, i.e., Muslims, while the other nationalities will have civic rights accorded to them as national minorities, under the prevailing international conventions; the Muslim state will have a Muslim ideology, founded on Islam and on Islamic legal-religious principles, but with those elements of a Western European provenance which are not in opposition to the above; a Muslim ideology will be built into the complete civic and legal system of the future Muslim state, into the state itself and its national symbols, through national policy matters, education, social and economic institutions—and, of course, the Muslim family, the nucleus of the whole state—and so on.[22]

For further encouragement of such a Bosniak-Islamic ethno-legal state, see the public declarations of Mirnes Ajanović.[23]

The concept of a Bosniak-Muslim republic was even included in the Bosnian Croatian-Bosniak Muslim peace agreement signed in Bonn on 9 January 1994. This agreement, in fact, is the most complete demonstration so far of the model for slicing Bosnia-Herzegovina into three parts. It even mentions a Bosniak-Muslim republic and the "Croatian Republic of Herceg-Bosna."

This reduction of an internationally recognized state to its "Muslim element" provided the fullest justification for the establishment of Croatian and Serbian parastate structures, and opened the doors to genocide.

Support for this "Muslim state" is growing among Bosniaks. Their question—a Muslim state, why not?—requires a cool-headed reply. Acceptance of such a possibility means, above all else, adopting the goals of the warmongers. This option, which the aggressors themselves admitted would be unpalatable

---

21. This position was expressed in an interview by E. H. Milharčić in *Mladina* (Ljubljana), 28 December 1993. E. Duraković said, among other things: "Now we don't want a multinational, multiconfessional Bosnian Republic of the kind which they have tried to force on us."

22. A. Jahić, "The Moral Muslim State," in *Zmaj od Bosne* (Tuzla), 27 September 1993. The text is reprinted in a pamphlet by F. Alispahić, *Krv boje benzina* [Blood the color of petrol] (Tuzla, 1996), 248–51. The article defines itself as an ideological blueprint for the desired "Muslim State."

23. See M. Ajanović, *Manifest bošnjačke republike* [Manifesto of a Bosniak republic] (Tuzla, 1995).

for the Bosniaks, could be transformed into good—or so its advocates believe. But this is an unfounded, ideologically driven picture, in which the fact that the fate of the Bosniaks is indivisible from Bosnia-Herzegovina as a whole has slipped out of sight. Division means ghettoization and will provide further opportunity for neighboring states to test its borders again and again. Accepting territorial enclosure and abandoning unity in multiplicity will not help the Bosniaks gain the resilience needed for survival. In any case, this option is no choice at all for those who have been forced to part with their inheritance. The "Muslim state" closes the door to the return of refugees, thus denying the most fundamental of human rights. In addition, it opens the way to greater subservience to ideological dogma—whereas what Bosnia's people most urgently need at this moment is freedom from such dogma.

11

In the public statements surrounding the plan to dismantle Bosnia as a historical and political unit and annex its parts to two new states, Greater Serbia and Greater Croatia, the underlying goal was deliberately kept vague. The plan's success is seen as a consequence of the inevitable "collapse" of Bosnian unity, inevitable because its people "cannot and will not live together any longer." But instead of explicitly stating any strategy or goal, the plan's advocates merely repeat that the Bosnian state cannot survive, owing to the lack of strong ties between its separate elements. There never has been any genuine unity, nor is there now, say the spokesmen of Greater Serbia and Greater Croatia. At the same time, untruths are being spread about Bosnian history and "the Muslim peril."

Various methods and resources were used to reach the final goal. These included, above all, the military might of the Yugoslav National Army (JNA), and a wealth of information, financial, diplomatic, economic, and other local and international networks inherited from former Yugoslavia. And since the mixed nature of Bosnia-Herzegovina's settlement was the main obstacle to the establishment of "homogeneous territories," genocide was a key component of the plan from the beginning.

From the beginning of 1992 until the end of the war in 1995, it is possible—taking the accepted definition of genocide—to say that genocide was carried out in the literal sense of the word on approximately 77 percent of Bosnia-

Herzegovina's territory. Every campaign of genocide requires four components: a ruling elite, an ideology, a political organization, and perpetrators. Let
us look at each of these elements in turn.

Genocide was carried out first in the areas that were defined in the course of
1991 as "Serbian autonomous regions" and next in those described as "Croatian national regions." The overall plan to destroy Bosnia-Herzegovina had initially two faces: one Serbian and one Croatian. Thus the ruling elite at the apex
of the genocidal pyramid can be seen as the double manifestation of a single
purpose.

The first element in the genocidal matrix was the plan hatched by the
Greater Serbian ruling elite personified primarily by Milošević, and its response was the Greater Croatian plan, hatched by Tuđman and his own ruling
elite. Both elites set up their own political and military superstructure among
the Bosnian Serbs and Croats, binding them to the respective state establishments of these two countries while assuring them of apparent independence.

The story fabricated for the benefit of the international community was that
the political survival of Bosnia-Herzegovina wholly depended on establishing
an agreement between "the three warring factions." This was accompanied by
the ruthless destruction of all political and cultural links that ensured Bosnia-
Herzegovina's unity as a state. In the face of such a resolute and aggressive
campaign, the response of the international community was to sue for peace
through deconstruction. Thus the basic goal of Milošević and Tuđman gained
respectability, and the forces of destruction and genocide were sheltered under
the wing of "peace efforts."

Meanwhile, as the desire for peace grew all the more desperate, the concentration camps, the massacres, the destruction of all traces of "other" cultures in
occupied areas, the expulsion of the survivors, and so on, grew apace. Not one
of these crimes would have been possible at any time during the war against
Bosnia without the express participation of the ethno-national elites in Belgrade and Zagreb, as clearly exhibited in the numerous statements issued by
their two leaders. Slobodan Milošević revealed this, when the greater part of
his goals had already been achieved via genocide, in the form of a letter from
the Serbian government of Serbia to his Bosnian stooges:

Serbia has endured huge numbers of victims to help you preserve freedom
and justice and create the Republika Srpska. It is not fair that Serbia and the
whole of Yugoslavia should still be waiting for the removal of sanctions
now, when all this has been achieved. If, after all this, you are so blinded by
selfish and personal interests, and if it is not enough for you to have estab-

lished the Republika Srpska on half of the territory of Bosnia-Herzegovina, and to have peace offered you on this basis, then you are on the most direct possible road to committing a crime against your own nation by refusing such a peace.[1]

It may be possible to argue that some factors in the implementation of genocide against the Bosniaks lay outside the initial decisions orchestrated by Zagreb and Belgrade. But it is clear that the decisions to establish concentration camps, to carry out acts of mass slaughter and expulsion, and to destroy everything Bosniak in every occupied city, town, and village, could not have been passed without the explicit involvement of these two powerful men. The war against Bosnia was orchestrated and directed according to their will, and with their full participation. Their continuing presence in the political arena shows that they are still committed to the achievement of their own goals in the areas politically and militarily bound to them.

The ideology that these elites use as their raison d'être has two elements: the Serbian element, which provided the original impetus, and the Croatian element, which responded to it. Both agree that Bosnia is a "false creation" that originally belonged to the Serbs and the Croats. Therefore the policies of Milošević and Tuđman and their cronies claim the moral and legal obligation to ensure the full protection of the Bosnian Serbs and Croats respectively. From this founding ideology it follows that the enmities and conflicts in the geopolitical territory to which it lays claim can be solved permanently by confirming clear borders between two new states, one for all Serbs and one for all Croats. So all Bosnian Serbs owe a duty of allegiance to Milošević, and all Bosnian Croats to Tuđman.

The anti-Bosnian plan formed and implemented by Croatian ethno-national policy is a mirror-image of its counterpart in Greater Serbian ideology. Although its regional interests are different, it is of the same vintage and design as the plan for Greater Serbia, its key ally. The views of Stevan Moljević, advocate of Greater Serbia and self-proclaimed Četnik ideologist before and during the Second World War, regarding a homogeneous Serbia apply as readily to Tuđman as they do to Milošević. "Therefore the Serbs are guided today by a primary and essential duty: to create and organize a homogeneous Serbia, which covers the whole ethnic region in which Serbs live. . . . Re-settlement

1. Letter of Slobodan Milošević to the Bosnian Serbs, published in *Politika* (Belgrade), 31 July 1994, 1.

and the exchange of homes, especially by Croats in Serbian areas and vice versa, is the only way to draw up a clear border and to create better relations."[2]

Both ruling elites see the Muslims as the only obstacle to this solution, which would otherwise win immediate sympathy among the great powers of the new world order: hence the strategy of presenting the Bosniaks as connected with elements unacceptable to these powers. So, while preparing the destruction of Bosnia, they encouraged and supported those Muslims whose political, ideological and cultural model of Islam was of the kind most alien to Europe. It is a little-known but remarkable fact that the "Islamic Mujahaddin," a favorite bogey of the West, found their way into Bosnia when the country was totally closed, under siege from East and West. They somehow managed to slip in at a time when the Bosnian-Herzegovinan government could not bring in so much as a truckload of food, let alone defense materials, except with Croatian connivance or consent. Moreover, the most authentic-looking bearded and turbaned Mujahaddin, operating across central Bosnia, are known to have been connected with the presence of the French security services—a fact supported by published and unchallenged evidence.[3]

This may also help to explain the arrival of Iranian help in Bosnia while all entry and exit points were, without exception, under the surveillance of the international community, whose troops were present in all war zones. Instead of acknowledging the traditional right of an attacked state to defend itself, the leading Western nations opened the doors to Iranian activity in Bosnia. Ironically, in so doing they put themselves at risk by flirting with what they themselves saw as a major international threat.

Thus a new scene unfolded in the Bosnian drama. The Western security services and media immediately started talking of "Islamic militants," "Islamic terrorism," "Islamic fundamentalism," and so on. Anything in European history which could be presented as an episode in the long struggle against Islam was dished up for local and international consumption, along with images and stereotypes from ethno-national myth. These depicted Muslims as the evil

2. S. Moljević, "Homogena Srbija" [A homogenous Serbia], manifesto published in "Zbornik dokumenata i podataka o narodnooslobodilačkom ratu naroda Jugoslavije" [A selection of documents and information about the war for national liberation of the Yugoslav peoples], XIV, Book I, *Dokumenti četničkog pokreta Draže Mihailovića 1941–1942,* Vojnoistorijski institut [Documents of the Četnik movement of Draža Mihailović, the Military-Historical Institute] (Belgrade, 1981), 1–10; the excerpts are taken from a reprint of this document in *Izvori velikosrpske agresije: rasprave, dokumenti, kartograf ski prikazi* [Sources of the greater Serbian aggression, discussions, documents, cartographic evidence], edited by B. Čović (Zagreb, 1991), 141.

3. See the letter in *Oslobođenje* of 7 October 1996, titled "Drapsi kao mudžahedini," by journalist Alda Radaelli.

Other, the embodiment of primitivism and inhumanity. The entire Bosnian-Herzegovinan state was reduced to this image of the Bosniaks: Muslims in the most negative sense, opposed to the civilized virtues of European culture.

The organizational structure necessary for the implementation of genocide can be found in the links that circumvented Bosnia-Herzegovina's constitutional order so as to derive their life-blood from Serbia and Croatia. The parastates these links produced, known as the "republics" of Srpska and Herceg-Bosna, are still organically connected to the power structures of Milošević and Tuđman.

The perpetrators of genocide, the torturers and executioners in the prison camps, those who destroyed mosques and churches, those who drove people out of their homes, were recruited mainly from the criminal elements in society. The impression of absolute power and invincibility given by the ruling elites, the spread of genocidal ideology, fine tuned for different social classes, via press, television, and radio, and the highly visible participation of the army, police, security services, and suchlike gave the campaign popular support. The campaign of killings, expulsions, and mass detentions, and the destruction of buildings and historic monuments would not have been possible, in other words, without the systematic and preplanned support of the ruling elites in Croatia and Serbia, and the organizations behind them.

To all these causes should be added the prevailing mentality of blind obedience to authority. Ethno-national identity meant loyalty to ethno-national leaders and was thus absorbed into the structure of genocide. People who might have raised conscientious objections were not usually involved in the crimes. They were relatively distant from the horrors of murder, torture, and mass expulsion. But their support for the state establishment that conducted the campaign was shown by the fact that they still acknowledged the authority of the leaders, backed up by the presence and—all too often—silence of the international community: "They will feel doubly absolved from responsibility. First, legitimate authority has given full warrant for their actions. Second, they have not themselves committed brutal physical acts."[4]

The whole campaign was carefully programmed in order to motivate large numbers of people to commit crimes. Social psychology dictated how this should be done: to absolve everyone of responsibility for their own actions; to render crime so routine that it no longer seems like crime; to use propaganda to make the victims of the crimes seem the guilty ones; and above all to ensure intense pressure from the social group. Every individual must feel that he or

4. S. Milgram, *Obedience to Authority: An Experimental View* (New York, 1974), 122.

she has no choice, or not be aware that there is a choice, when obedience is demanded.

Genocide was a necessary element in the destruction of Bosnia-Herzegovina.[5] The Greater Serbian and Greater Croatian ruling elites saw the Bosniaks, together with those Bosnian Croats and Bosnian Serbs who proved resistant to the call of ethno-nationalism, as the main obstacle to dividing and "tidying up" the country. The Bosniaks, therefore, had to be turned against the idea of Bosnian-Herzegovinan unity and forced, where possible, to set up systems that aped those of their persecutors. They could then be relied upon to alienate or destroy any Bosnian Serbs and Croats who retained pro-Bosnian feelings and persisted in living as part of a mixed community.

Abandoning the idea of Bosnian-Herzegovinan unity, the Bosniaks thus became the "third party to the conflict," blindly obedient to the infallible authority of their own leadership. Such a leadership, because it never makes mistakes, has the right to make whatever decisions it likes. The possibility of a conscience-guided choice was reduced even further by the apparently hostile or indifferent policy of the West, the fact that the impossibility of living together was proclaimed by all sides, and the relentless promotion of the superficial differences between cultures. Simultaneously, of course, the living nucleus of their population was being wiped out of existence.

Bosniak ethno-national ideology is as sharply divided from Bosnia-Herzegovina's actual history as its Serbian and Croatian counterparts and tends toward a closed and formalist understanding of the Islamic tradition. Such an ideology seeks its supporters and advocates from within religious structures. The evil nature of this ideology is evident in the attacks made on individuals and groups who think differently: they are called "demons," *izmet* (excrement), and so on.

This attitude and these opinions are no more than a parody of the ideology of the criminals. This enables the perpetrators to stress that the victims deserved or brought about their own fates, thus enabling them to hide or justify their crimes, as the rot spreads on all sides. Thus a dangerous "Muslim collectivism," devoid of moral content, sprang up as a backlash to the crimes committed against Bosnia.

Confronted by the indisputable decay of the Bosnian-Herzegovinan state,

---

5. Serious examinations of these phenomena of genocide have been presented in several books, the following of which are especially worthy of mention: R. Gutman, *A Witness to Genocide* (New York, 1993); N. Cigar, *Genocide in Bosnia: The Policy of "Ethnic Cleansing"* (Texas, 1995); *Genocid u Bosni i Hercegovini od 1991. do 1995. godine, Zbornik radova* [Genocide in Bosnia and Herzegovina from 1991 to 1995], edited by S. Čekić (Sarajevo, 1998).

and the impossibility of explaining this without some sort of logical model, Alija Izetbegović announced: "The main danger for Bosnia is Serbian and Croatian extremism, and after that Muslim."[6] In this statement, the first such statement in the whole of his political career, Izetbegović finally acknowledged the destructive nature of "Muslim extremism." The word "extremism," in fact, alludes to an entire hierarchy of leaders, ideologies, organizations, and individual perpetrators. The Greater Serbian and Greater Croatian plans have been joined by a Bosniak or Muslim plan with the same structure.

6. A. Izetbegović, New Year press conference, *Dnevni avaz* (Sarajevo), 27 December 1997, 5.

12

THE CHRIST KILLERS

All Bosniak presence has been erased from around 75 percent of Bosnia-Herzegovina's territory. The process was one of systematic slaughter, expulsion, and destruction of buildings, property, and historic monuments. Taking the mass of evidence together with the accepted definition of genocide, no doubt can remain that what was committed against the Bosniak people was genocide in the full sense of the term. It is understandable, but not acceptable, why this fact did not provoke decisive counteraction on the part of the international powers. As their acknowledgment and response lagged so far behind the disclosure of the facts, they must accept a measure of guilt and responsibility for what happened. What the situation demands from them is justice, which is significantly more difficult than merely expressing pity and concern for the numbers killed and the devastation of the country.

Justice, moreover, has been hampered further by the peace plan and its implementation, which exclude a number of ways of dealing with the forces that planned and carried out the genocide. Meanwhile, there is an ongoing demand for the reaffirmation of regional efforts to implement the concepts and elements of "liberal democracy" and "Christianity" within the framework of the new ethno-national ideologies.

Opposition to Communist ideology and its totalitarian system of government found significant encouragement and support in the tenets of liberal democracy and the achievements of Western free enterprise. Demands for religious freedom, as opposed to the aggressive atheism of the ruling ideology, were the most convincing form of open disagreement with and opposition to totalitarianism. This type of protest was fundamentally linked to the latter's destruction, since its demands could claim to be on behalf of the entire nation, whereas those linked with the need for democratic transformation were confined to a small and controversial political and intellectual elite.

Calls for religious freedom having become an essential part of any political action against the ruling system, the link between religious education and ethno-national ideology revealed itself in the identification of religious freedom with ethno-national freedom. When criticizing the Communist government, ethno-national deprivation was regularly emphasized, which always implied religious deprivation. "How can we live," Dobrica Ćosić demanded, "so deprived of our civic and national rights, so humiliated?" He went on to ask about "the wounds that are inflicted on us and that we bear" and "the injustice that we have suffered and are suffering."[1]

In this way social facts were translated, using religious symbols and traditions, into an historical image of evil and suffering, which required a final and immediate solution in the present. Freedom from this humiliation and healing for these wounds can be found, according to this philosophy, in democratization and spiritual renewal. However, these principles can rapidly turn into ethno-national bigotry, which, on meeting opposition, attacks it as an enemy or accuses it of revisionism. Religious elements are included, not for their own sake, but to promote the new ideology. Total submission is demanded from religion. Ethno-national goals are presented as the only ones powerful enough to overcome the old totalitarian mentality and social inertia. Therefore they need the appeal of religion, but also aid the interests of the church establishment.

As for society, it must be redefined in order to sow hatred and conflict among those who are destined by the ethno-national plan to split into separate states. Establishing these new ethno-national states can be achieved, as Ćosić suggests, through separation, "so that we do away with reasons for hating and killing each other."[2] "It would be possible," he believes, "to have planned resettlement and the exchange of homes, which would be highly painful and difficult, but better than living in hatred and mutual killing."[3]

1. Quoted in N. Popov, *Srpska strana rata: trauma i katarza u istorijskom pamćenju* [The Serbian side of the war: Trauma and catharsis in historic memory] (Belgrade, 1996), 384, 385.
2. Ibid., 331.
3. Ibid., 338. This view of hatred as a core element of the Bosnian being results from opposition to diversity as a sacred demonstration of Unity on the one hand, and from national ideologies which demand "homogeneity" on the other. Plans for a "homogeneous Serbia" or "homogeneous Croatia," in their worst form, meet their direct antithesis in Bosnia. No part of the Bosnian model is hated so much as its unity in diversity. This hatred as a subject of national ideologies, however, is displayed as the alleged content of

According to this reading, living together means hatred and killing: this can be solved only by removing the cause. All ideological images of interethnic hatred illustrate this basic premise. Those who stand for communal life, accordingly, are supporters of hatred and killing. The goal is the new ethno-national state, which can only be created by dividing up the people. So greater hatred and greater killing are necessary to support this goal. The result is a paradox: opposing the totalitarian system to bring about democratic change means promising new ethno-national states, which leads to the justification of immense hatred and mass murder. The goal is held to be "good," but its achievement is only possible through a relentless urging and encouragement of crime.

Thus we come nearer to understanding the new "anti-ideological" ideology of the ethno-national state. Talk of democratization and uprooting totalitarianism is mere rhetoric, which aims to clear the way to a new ideological goal in which the ethno-religious and ethno-national elites are united. This policy tries to equate itself with religious faith, as the Orthodox churchman Božidar Mijač makes clear: "All the tragic events in national history, and especially recent one, . . . should be considered as part of our sacred striving toward the Kingdom of Heaven."[4]

---

the hated object, in this case Bosnia. Neither Ćosić nor Tuđman know anything about Bosnia. Their hatred springs from their blind allegiance to national ideology and their frenzied desire for ethno-national homogeneity. Ćosić repeats his story of hatred just as long as is needed to produce a history which accords with his ideology. What he comes up with is nothing but a false reading of the false reading of history produced by Ivo Andrić. There is nothing coincidental about the fact that Ivo Andrić, in his short story about hatred. "Pismu iz 1920. godine" [Letter from 1920], speaks through the speech and writings of Dr. Maks Levenfeld: "Max Levenfeld, a doctor's son. Born and raised in Sarajevo, where he had built up a large practice. Jewish in origin, long since converted. His mother was born in Trieste, the daughter of an Italian baroness and an Austrian naval officer, himself the descendant of French emigres. In Sarajevo, two generations remembered her figure, her bearing, and her elegant style of dress. She was marked by the kind of beauty respected and appreciated by people otherwise quite impudent and vulgar."

Yet this is not Dr. Levenfeld talking, but the bitter heirs of "homogeneous nations." Just as the hater transfers his hatred to the hated object, so the heirs of ethno-national ideology find their spokesmen only where it is least probable, for in this way they can convince themselves. Therefore, Ćosić and his counterparts recognize the words of their faith in the statement of Levenfeld: "Bosnia is a country of hatred and fear." The superficial image of the striking of midnight among the Sarajevo steeples is offered as a means for the transference of hatred: "Thus at night while everyone is sleeping, division keeps vigil in the counting of the late, small hours, and separates these sleeping people who, when awake, rejoice and mourn, feast and fast by four different and antagonistic calendars, and send all their prayers and wishes to one heaven, in four different liturgical languages. And this difference, sometimes visible and open, sometimes invisible and hidden, is always similar to hatred, and often completely identical with it" (I. Andrić, *Deca* [Children] [Sarajevo, 1976], 186). This interpretation of multiplicity is divorced from its essence. For manifestations to become like this, first of all the center and the connections through which they are only signs of the One and the Same would have to die inside them. (For the incoherence underlying this interpretation of multiplicity, see also I. Lovrenović, *Bosna, kraj stoljeća* [Bosnia, the end of the century] [Zagreb, 1996], 16, 38–39.)

4. Quoted in Popov, *Srpska strana rata,* 278.

Supporting an explicit plan for geopolitical redefinition of the states comprising Yugoslavia, Patriarch Pavle wrote to Peter Carrington in October 1991: "It is time to understand that the victims of genocide, and their former, and perhaps their future, conquerors, cannot live together."[5] (By "victims of genocide" he was referring to the Serbian nation.)

When the war against Bosnia-Herzegovina was already well under way, Božidar Mijač, quoted above, claimed that peace and justice are on the sides "of those who defend their soul, country and faith; and not of those who destroy another's soul, country and faith, who, in times past and present, have ravaged the long-suffering Serbian lands with genocidal crimes."[6]

At the beginning of 1994, when a considerable amount of murder, expulsion, and partition had already been committed, Radovan Karadžić declared, "Our faith is present in all our thinking and decisions, and the voice of the Church is obeyed as the voice of supreme authority."[7]

In such an ethno-national ideology, relations toward other ethnic groups are viewed through the medium of archetypal religious symbols. The "historic suffering" of the Serbian nation is trotted out onto the political stage to play the role of sanctifying ethno-national goals, along with calls for democratic transformation and the struggle against totalitarian ideology. This suffering is linked with the Passion of Christ. Thus, at the level of popular thinking, the battle for the "sacred" ethno-national goal—that is, the construction of a new ethno-national state possible only through the destruction of Bosnia-Herzegovina—is identified with the suffering undergone by Christ himself. This automatically establishes the guilt of all those who oppose the ethno-national plan, of all those who do not accept the splitting of their country for the sake of the goal proclaimed by ethno-national propaganda. Their opposition can immediately be seen as a denial of faith.

This view appears repeatedly in different phrasings, showing that those holding it wanted to convince everybody, perhaps even the victims, that the killings were not only justified by the "sacred" ethno-national goal of the executioners, but were even good for the victims themselves.

The celebration of Good Friday is supposed to involve the Christian believer more deeply in Christ's suffering on the Cross.[8] The Messiah is betrayed

5. Ibid., 291.
6. Ibid., 294.
7. Ibid., 300.
8. Good Friday precedes Easter. It is traditionally the day of Christ's passion. Both Roman Catholics and many Protestants take part in a service of remembrance of Christ's suffering between noon and three in the afternoon. (see Matthew 27:45; Mark 15:33; Luke 23:44).

and delivered to his killers. The crowd cries out "His blood be on us and on our children" (Matthew 27:25). Struggling to Calvary with the cross on which he will be broken, Christ passes people who, by their silence or mockery, made themselves accomplices in his death. As he foretold, he is betrayed by one of his own disciples, Judas Iscariot, who listens to Christ's proclamation of the "glad tidings" and eats with him at the same table. The traitor and the killers came from the same stock. A model of eternal conflict is created: between the followers of Christ, who are essentially good, and his betrayers and murderers, who embody all evil.

The Church teaches that Christ was cruelly murdered. His suffering is the central question of all human existence, for it opens the gate to salvation: acceptance of this is the first step toward salvation. Meditating, every Good Friday, on Christ's suffering means simultaneously meditating on his betrayers, torturers, and killers. Contemplation of Christ in the context of his suffering increases one's awareness of those responsible for this suffering. The Passion can be, and has been, used at many times and places to reinforce the individual's duty to confront the new incarnations of his killers. Historical examples of its use as propaganda range from the campaigns of expulsion and killing directed against various Christian sects in Europe, the persecution and killing of Muslims and Jews together in Spain, Sicily, and elsewhere, and the widespread persecution of Jews throughout Europe, culminating in the Holocaust of the twentieth century.[9]

The centerpiece of the Serbian national plan, propagandized as a focus of national feeling, was the Battle of Kosovo.[10] This incorporates the classic contrast between the Christian knights of the Serbian Kingdom on the one hand and the Muslim aggressors on the other. Prince Lazar's last supper represents the last supper of Christ with his disciples. Lazar is the Serbian incarnation of

9. For further light on this topic, see C. Roth, "The medieval conception of the Jew," in *Essays and Studies in Memory of Linda R. Miller,* edited by I. Davidson (New York, 1938), 171–90; J. Cohen, *The Friars and the Jews: the Evolution of Medieval Anti-Judaism* (Ithaca, 1992); J. Cohen, "The Jews as killers of Christ in the Latin tradition, from Augustine to the Friars," *Traditio* 29 (1983): 1–28; for a mor comprehensive overview of the ideological and institutional relationships underlying the persecution, see R. I. Moore, *The Formation of a Persecuting Society* (New York, 1987); and Gavin Langmuir, *History, Religion and Antisemitism* (Berkeley, 1990). The connection between anti-Muslim and anti-Jewish prejudice is studied in A. Cutler and H. Cutler's book, *The Jew as an Ally of the Muslim* (Southbend, 1986). The connection between the genocide in Bosnia and the notion of Christ's Killers is analyzed in Michael A. Sells' book, *The Bridge Betrayed: Religion and Genocide in Bosnia* (Berkeley, 1996).

10. The demand for the reshaping of Yugoslavia, as set out in the *Memorandum Srpske akademije nauka i umetnosti* [Memorandum of the Serbian Academy of the Sciences and Arts] (1986). Here there is evidence that the movement against Bosnia-Herzegovina is also linked with Kosovo. Ćosić said in 1987 that Kosovo is "our heaviest national defeat since 1813" (quoted in Popov, *Srpska strana rata,* 386).

Christ, facing up to his killers through his acceptance of his destiny. Siding with Lazar means siding with Christ, and the battle against Muslims is the battle against the killers of Christ. There is even a Serb Judas in this myth: Vuk Branković, who betrayed the Serbian nation by joining with the killers.

Thus a coherent, all-embracing pattern is created, by which Muslims should be viewed: they are Christ's killers, and those Serbs who continue living with them are Christ's betrayers.[11] This pattern is prevalent in the mainstream of Serbian culture and forms a key component of the national plan. Its most explicit champions are Vuk Stefanović Karadžić, the nineteenth-century "father of the Serbian language," with his theories of the Serbian language as the definer of Serbian national territory and of the folk-epic inheritance as the foundation for a nationalized popular consciousness. The pattern is crystallized in "The Mountain Wreath," by the nineteenth-century Montenegrin bishop Petar Petrović Njegoš: the message conveyed by this seminal poetic drama is that the battle between Serbs and Muslims is the battle between good and evil and can only end in the destruction of one or the other: "Our battle shall have no end / Until we or the Turks are dead to the last man."[12]

The pattern has its archetypal reflection in a more recent episode: the destruction of Yugoslavia is generally recognized to have been ignited by Milošević's infamous 1989 rally in Kosovo, on the six-hundredth anniversary of the battle. Here posters were sold bearing icon-style portraits of Christ, Prince Lazar, and Milošević, side by side in a kind of holy trinity.[13]

The destruction of everything and everyone Muslim— male and female, young and old—the eradication of all reminders of their existence—graves and mosques, houses and bridges—is proclaimed to be a sacred act that deserves sacred praise, as symbolized by the blessings bestowed on the crusading killers by Bishop Danilo at the end of "The Mountain Wreath." Lazar's "Last Summons" and his Last Supper demand a response from all who identify the Kosovo catastrophe with the torment of Christ, for "he who does not take revenge cannot become blest" (*ko se ne osveti, taj se ne posveti*).

Though the model of "we" as Christ's followers or even His likeness[14] and

---

11. See *Pravoslavlje,* the newspaper of the Serbian Orthodox Church, 15 May 1993: "The Serbian army in the Republika Srpska is fighting under its national tricolour, has entered the heart of Orthodox tradition, is seeking its models in our national heroes" (quoted in Popov, *Srpska strana rata,* 298–99).

12. Petar II P. Njegoš, *Gorski vijenac* [Mountain wreath] (Belgrade, 1984), 17. The ideologues of Greater Serbia call all Balkan Muslims "Turks." The equation of Muslims with Turks was used in the Anti-Bosnia-Herzegovina War from 1991 to 1995.

13. See N. Malcolm, *Bosnia: A Short History* (London, 1996), 213.

14. At a Serbian Democratic Party (SDS) rally held in Sarajevo's Zetra stadium, Radovan Karadžić during his speech: "Tonight even God is a Serb!"

"they" as Christ's killers is present in Serbian culture, it was specifically targeted and promoted as a key element in the preparations for a Greater Serbia. It rapidly became central to the actions of the organizers and perpetrators of genocide in Bosnia. Everything Muslim was proclaimed evil and unworthy even to exist. Thus Bishop Atanasije of Herzegovina-Zahum castigated the traditional Turkish-style architecture—houses with internal courtyards and high external walls—as the sign of "Islamic primitivism from Bihać to Baghdad and Belgrade."[15] Metropolitan Nikolaj, the primate of the Orthodox Church in Bosnia, proclaimed at Easter 1993, while standing between Radovan Karadžić and Ratko Mladić, that accepting the leadership of these two men meant "following the difficult road of Christ."[16] In 1993, the Greek Orthodox church bestowed its highest honor on Karadžić, the nine-hundred-year-old Order of Saint Dionysius of Chankeia, proclaiming him to be "one of the most outstanding sons of our Lord Jesus Christ who labors for peace."[17]

Thus, destroying everything Muslim, as comprehensively and cruelly as possible, was portrayed as an act of allegiance to the Serbian ideal and simultaneously to Christ. The perpetrators of these crimes were systematically brainwashed into regarding the Muslim presence as an evil phenomenon that deserved no less than total destruction. The torturers and killers became, through their criminal rampage, the preservers of the Serbian holy of holies.

All these aspects of the anti-Bosnian/anti-Bosniak/anti-Muslim campaign within the framework of the Greater Serbian Plan are prominent in the Greater Croatian Plan, which evolved in reaction to the former, and in the numerous Croatian variants of anti-Bosnianism, anti-Bosniakism, and anti-Islamicism. Neither could have succeeded so extensively without the backup provided by the other. Both employed a portrayal of Muslim and Bosniak policy that justified the basic premise of both plans and that was displayed to the international community as a dangerous and repulsive manifestation that had to be stopped by all available means. These anti-Bosnia-Herzegovina, anti-Bosniak, and anti-Muslim plans enjoyed their greatest success, however, when Muslim religious denominationalism became the core of a Bosniak national ideology. When religion is reduced to an absolutist interpretation of religious concepts and symbols—except for those elements which, whether through Christ or Muhammad, demonstrate its underlying unity—the ground is prepared for the development of separate entities whose foundation rests on hatred.

15. R. Radivojić, *Intervju* (Belgrade), 9 December 1988, 27.

16. Sells, *The Bridge Betrayed,* 81–82.

17. E. Sorel, "Religion in the News," *The Nation,* 11 October 1993, 380; see also M. Peretz, "Cape Cod Diarist: Symbolic Politics," *The Nation,* 5 September 1994, 50.

By responding in this way, the Bosnian Muslims turned their own thoughts and actions into the mirror-image of what was being used so successfully against them. One could quote a host of examples of reactions by Bosniak politicians that exactly mirror anti-Bosnian propaganda. This dangerously obscures Bosniak national policy, transforming it from straightforward self-defense into something unpleasantly like the promotion of hatred to obtain political goals.

13

THE MUTILATION OF THE STATE

Bosnia has developed a unique national identity and culture over approximately one thousand years. The latest war was possibly the greatest upheaval ever to take place in Bosnia's evolution through unity in diversity, and it assailed all aspects of the country of Bosnia-Herzegovina. Its unity had remained constant despite earlier fluctuations of border and government, retrospectively distorted though it was from time to time by ideologized versions of history. The presence and impact of Christian debate and conflict, the schism that divided the Greco-Roman inheritance, the religious traditions outside the official churches, and other factors demand fresh research. The truth about Bosnia will be accessible only if these and other phenomena are placed in their proper context in European history—including the role of viewpoints, symbols, and interpretations widespread throughout Europe but of non-European origin. Bosnia is a microcosm of Europe's complexity. Contemporary "local" issues or events cannot be understood in isolation from the whole European cultural and historical web.

The internal differences that seemed to play such a key role in the drama of war were forced into doing so by the actions of Bosnia's powerful neighbors. These dealings aimed at creating and promoting a model of a country split by irreconcilable internal differences. A campaign was set up to stimulate the differences and suppress all forces for tolerance and mutual trust. The concentrated use of brute force by the politico-military establishment was also required to shatter Bosnia's unity. All rules of war were bent or flouted because the attackers were not only concerned with taking territory. The Greater Serbian and Greater Croatian plans can be summed up by citing their two most immediate purposes: the establishment of ethno-national rule in their respective territories, once cleansed of Bosniak presence, and the destruction of Bosnia-Herzegovina in terms of its significance as a common state for members of all ethno-national groups. Destruction was justified by appeals to historical, legal, ethnic, and ideological criteria, geopolitical law, and, as a last resort, the principle that might is right.

There are many examples of the denial of Bosnian-Herzegovinan statehood on the basis of geopolitical law distorted in support of ethno-national goals. They always follow the same pattern.

> Does Croatia have the right to assume such a geographical shape as will enable her survival? Of course she does. For Croatia with cancer in her womb—or even without a womb, for the Serbs and the Muslims have taken it—cannot exist long-term, never mind for ever. Therefore she has a right to Bosnia-Herzegovina, regardless of who may have lived in Bosnia-Herzegovina, Croats and whoever else. As for the fate of the nations who live there but are not Croats, these nations themselves will decide. If they are loyal to the Croatian state they can live there in peace, and if they are not they will suffer all the consequences of disloyalty. [1]

Throughout history, the inhabitants of Bosnia-Herzegovina have differed in their religious allegiance. Only in the last two centuries has this difference been declared to be a "national"—that is, ethnic—one. The members of the three peoples that constitute the Bosnian-Herzegovinan nation lived intermingled throughout the region, living proof of unity in diversity. According to a census held in 1991, Bosniaks made up 44 percent of the total inhabitants and lived on 94 percent of the territory; Croats represented 17 percent of the population and lived on 70 percent of the territory; Serbs made up 41 percent and lived on 95 percent of the territory. Nowhere had the principle of pure ethno-national or ethno-religious regions been established. Nor were there significant differences between regions, even at the geographical extremes of Bosnia's territory. This presented a serious obstacle to the establishment of ethno-national territories that could be divided into separate entities or transformed into new states: therefore, the Greater Serbian and Greater Croatian

---

1. P. Vučić, *Politička sudbina Hrvatske: geopolitičke i geostrateške karakteristike Hrvatske* (Zagreb, 1995), 300. Petar Vučić, a prominent geostrategic/political analyst, whose *Political Destiny of Croatia* was recommended reading for students of Zagreb's Faculty of Political Science.

plans required the destruction of existing patterns of settlement. This demanded the prolonged incitement of hatred on the basis of differences, followed by war, all of which was masterminded by external powers. The whole strategy underlying the war against Bosnia-Herzegovina from 1991 to 1995 was directed at destroying her unity in diversity.

The result of this strategy is clear if we look at the status of populations and cultural monuments in the three politico-military territories created by war and genocide:

DEMOGRAPHIC CHANGES AND TERRITORIAL DIVISIONS (1992-1996)

The data in the tables have been taken from unpublished research by I. Bošnjović, "Vojne teritorije i demografske promjene u Bosni i Hercegovini od 1992. do 1996. godine" (Sarajevo, 1997).

The Dayton Peace Agreement, by confirming the division of Bosnia-Herzegovina into two parts and the existence of three ethnic armies, one in one part and two in the other, accepted the consequences of war and genocide. In actual fact, the agreement on refugees and displaced persons, which is a component of the peace accord for Bosnia-Herzegovina, states that "all refugees and displaced persons have the right to freely return to their homes." The likelihood of the full implementation of this article is not great. But the survival of Bosnia and Herzegovina depends on it.

The internal borders established by the Dayton Agreement have nothing to do with the cultural and demographic development of Bosnia-Herzegovina. Settlement patterns and economic links were crudely broken apart by the newly imposed borders. The main axis along which the economic and demographic unity of Bosnia-Herzegovina had developed was the Bosanski Šamac-Doboj-Zenica-Sarajevo-Mostar-Čapljina line. Bosnia's social, cultural, and economic unity was bound to this axis. It was via this line that the country reached out to its southern and northern neighbors. Similarly, the Bosanska Gradiška-Banja Luka-Jajce-Travnik-Sarajevo line and the northern Bihać-Banja Luka-Prijedor-Doboj-Tuzla-Zvornik axis were both linked to this main axis.

Territory	Bosniaks	Croats	Serbs	Others	Total
	A. Population as of March 31, 1991				
HVO	120,704	353,215	83,807	28,206	585,932
B-H Army	1,312,959	255,081	397,383	196,041	2,161,464

Territory	Bosniaks	Croats	Serbs	Others	Total
A. Population as of March 31, 1991 (*continued*)					
Serbian Army	450,382	149,763	877,008	116,169	1,593,322
Total	1,884,045	758,059	1,358,198	340,416	4,340,718
B. Population as of March 31, 1992					
HVO	122,349	357,432	85,197	28,575	593,553
B-H Army	1,330,851	258,126	402,691	198,608	2,190,276
Serbian Army	466,011	151,147	887,443	122,622	1,627,223
Total	1,919,211	766,705	1,375,331	349,805	4,411,052
C. Resettled and refugee population, 1992–1996 (±)					
HVO	—	142,000	—	4,500	146,500
B-H Army	317,000	—	—	25,500	342,500
Serbian Army	—	—	205,000	20,000	225,000
Total	317,000	142,000	205,000	50,000	714,000
D. Natural population growth, 1992–1996 (±)					
HVO	600	7,500	400	106	8,606
B-H Army	39,400	1,400	1,800	734	43,334
Serbian Army	1,300	300	14,600	560	16,760
Total	41,300	9,200	16,800	1,400	68,700
E. Displaced and expelled population, 1992–1996 (-)					
HVO	32,000	—	43,000	9,000	84,000
B-H Army	—	80,000	162,000	19,000	261,000
Serbian Army	285,000	62,000	—	22,000	369,000
Total	317,000	142,000	205,000	50,000	714,000
F. Refugee population moved abroad, 1992–1996 (-)					
HVO	62,000	147,000	30,000	5,000	244,000
B-H Army	355,000	110,000	104,000	35,000	604,000
Serbian Army	108,000	67,000	218,000	56,000	449,000
Total	525,000	324,000	352,000	96,000	1,297,000
G. Missing, killed, and increase in death rate (-)					
HVO	8,300	19,700	1,200	980	30,180
B-H Army	102,400	4,300	5,900	7,080	119,680
Serbian Army	42,200	7,060	62,250	5,440	119,950
Total	152,900	31,060	72,350	13,500	269,810
H. Population in Bosnia-Herzegovina at the end of March, 1996[a]					
HVO	20,000	340,000	11,000	18,500	389,500
B-H Army	1,230,000	65,000	133,000	163,500	1,591,500
Serbian Army	32,000	15,000	823,500	60,000	930,500
Total	1,282,000	420,000	967,500	242,000	2,911,500
I. Displaced and relocated populations, 1992–1996					
HVO→ B-H Army	32,000	—	—	6,500	38,500
HVO→ Serbian Army	—	—	43,000	2,500	45,500

Territory	Bosniaks	Croats	Serbs	Others	Total
I. Displaced and relocated populations, 1992–1996 (*continued*)					
HVO→					
Croatia	1,000	52,000	—	500	53,500
HVO→					
Yugoslavia	300	—	21,000	1,000	22,300
B-H Army→					
HVO	60,700	95,000	9,000	3,500	168,200
B-H Army→					
HVO	—	80,000	—	1,500	81,500
B-H Army→					
Serbian Army	—	—	162,000	17,500	179,500
B-H Army→					
Croatia	15,000	36,000	—	3,500	54,500
B-H Army→					
Yugoslavia	5,000	—	78,000	7,000	90,000
B-H Army→					
Other countries	335,000	74,000	26,000	24,500	459,500
Serbian Army→					
HVO	—	60,500	—	3,000	63,500
Serbian Army→					
B-H Army	285,000	1,500	—	19,000	305,500
Serbian Army→					
Croatia	5,000	27,000	—	3,000	35,000
Serbian Army→					
Yugoslavia	1,000	—	170,000	15,000	186,000
Serbian Army→					
Other countries	102,000	40,000	48,000	38,000	228,000
Total	842,000	466,000	557,000	146,000	2,011,000
Croatia→					
Serbian Army	—	—	90,000	10,000	100,000
GRAND TOTAL	842,000	466,000	647,000	156,000	2,111,000

ª The summary of data from Tables B to H is given in this table. Insignificant differences in this summary are the result of rounding off.

The Dayton borders, drawn up in purely military, political, and ethnic terms, destroyed the centuries-old structures of settlement, micro- and macro-economy, and culture. Urban centers and their industrial suburbs were violently split apart and stripped of their basic preconditions for economic survival. The state's administrative basis—the four provinces of Banja Luka, Sarajevo-Zenica, Tuzla, and Mostar—was ripped apart, leaving it bereft of a regional infrastructure. Economic activity today is reduced in many areas to isolated pockets, while the Bosnian economy as a whole lacks the trade and other links, including basic transport systems and even freedom of movement, fundamental to economic growth. Regional connections and relationships have been utterly destroyed: this could have been prevented, had the designers of Dayton taken into account the prospect of reintegration while dreaming up these new borders.

Reintegration needs to take place on two levels. The restoration of internal links should be accompanied by measures to prevent the possibility of disruption on the part of the neighboring powers while reintegrating Bosnia-Herzegovina with its neighbors and its wider surroundings. The Dayton Agreement envisions a unified economic space that will be ensured by a unified monetary system. Such a structure is, however, opposed by the legislative, legal, and executive powers of the three regional entities. The original plans for the destruction of Bosnia-Herzegovina remained active after the signing of the Dayton Agreement, and their campaign to split Bosnia-Herzegovina continued. The goals are the same, only the means have changed. The envisaged linkages between one entity and the Republic of Croatia, and between the other entity and rump Yugoslavia (Serbia and Montenegro), can only weaken the external borders of Bosnia-Herzegovina and strengthen her internal borders. Today it is more clear than ever that the linkages between the two entities and Croatia and Serbia respectively are greater than those between the entities themselves.

Nevertheless, the division confirmed by the Dayton Agreement acknowledging two separate entities—the Federation of Bosnia-Herzegovina and the Republika Srpska—does not completely fulfill the original designs of Milošević and Tuđman. Therefore, Tuđman feels that the Western powers should allocate the Federation to the Republic of Croatia as a "protectorate." [2] This conviction forms part and parcel of his claim that the "Europeanizing" of the Muslims [3] is the task of Croatia.

2. See Chapter 8 note 3.

3. After the Croatian National Plan had resulted in the general expulsion of Muslim residents from all parts of Bosnia-Herzegovina that came under Croatian control and in the destruction of the main Bosniak cultural monuments in these areas, Tuđman told the paper *Le Figaro*, on 25 September 1995: "Croatia has undertaken the task of Europeanizing the Bosnian Muslims."

14

INCOMPATIBLE CIVILIZATIONS

The transformation of "the Yugoslav crisis" into "the drama of Bosnia-Herzegovina" and "the Muslim question" was based on the joint action plan of Milošević and Tuđman. This plan coincides at many points with the main features of the "conflict of civilizations" model offered to the world public in 1993 by Samuel Peter Huntington.[1] The logical bases for this model are close to, and often identical with, the efforts by the ethno-national elites of Bosnia-Herzegovina's neighbors to encourage and justify the destruction of Bosnia and Herzegovina. At the beginning of 1993, Dobrica Ćosić told the members of the Greek parliament: "Bosnia and Herzegovina is a complete sublimation of the historical antagonisms in this space—ethnic, religious, cultural, and political."[2] In his speech of 14 December 1995, on the occasion of signing the Dayton Peace Agreement, Tuđman said that Bosnia-Herzegovina was "divided for the most part by a conflict of civilization."[3] Compare the implications of these statements with the public announcement of Milošević and Tuđman on 25 March 1991 in Karađorđevo, when they "agreed that in the process of peacefully and democratically solving the Yugoslavian crisis, respect for the interests of the Serbian and Croatian nations as a whole must be

1. S. P. Huntington, "The Clash of Civilizations?" *Foreign Affairs* 72, no. 3 (summer 1993): 22–49; the contents of this article are developed further in the book *The Clash of Civilizations and the Remaking of World Order* (New York, 1996).
2. See Chapter 10 note 3.
3. Quoted in *Oslobođenje,* 12 December 1995, 4.

ensured,"[4] and, of course, Tuđman's pronouncements about "the unnatural shape of Croatia, . . . the little statelet of Bosnia, where Muslims would have the majority and form a buffer between Serbia and Croatia," and the disappearance of the "colonial creation of Bosnia-Herzegovina."[5] Such statements shrouded their anti-Bosnian and anti-Muslim designs behind the smoke screen of a "conflict of civilizations."

Milošević and Tuđman agreed on the redrawing of territories and resettlement of inhabitants that had to take place in order for the Bosnian-Herzegovinan state to disappear and be replaced by the expanded all-Croatian and all-Serbian states. This is how the goal of ensuring the interests of the Serbian and Croatian nations as a whole would be achieved. This agreement was laid before working parties, who met in Belgrade and Tikveš to reach a final agreement on "geographical delineations." This task was furthered by Radovan Karadžić and Mate Boban during their meetings in Graz and in Njivice in May and June 1992.

All these outline plans hinged on forcing the Muslims into a "Mini-Bosnia," the ghetto reserved for those Muslims who survived the genocide. Ironically, while measures were taking place to bring this about, including the eager encouragement of any wishes in this direction among the Muslim population, the Muslims were directly accused of wanting their own pure Islamic state. Thus the original goals of Milošević and Tuđman were imposed on the political thinking and actions of the Muslims themselves.

"The Muslims want," Tuđman explained, "to establish control over the whole of Mostar; next, to reach to the coast, and to establish an Islamic state. The Muslims consider that, only because they have the demographic majority in Bosnia, they can bring all her citizens under Islamic law—and this was actually why this conflict was started."[6] This key premise in the justification of his geopolitical and geostrategic goals and his intensified efforts for their achievement was to be repeated in February 1998: "We supported the foundation of the Croatian Republic of Herceg-Bosna so that we could protect the Croatian presence in a Bosnia-Herzegovina from which the Serbs had split, and in which the Muslims wanted to build their Muslim state in accordance with Koranic Muslim laws."[7]

But it was actually Tuđman and Milošević who came up with the sugges-

4. Quoted in *Oslobođenje*, 25 March 1991.
5. See Chapter 7 note 5.
6. From Tuđman's interview with *Der Spiegel*, 21 January 1995.
7. Tuđman's speech to the Fourth Congress of the Croatian Democratic Union (HDZ) as quoted by *Oslobođenje*, 23 February 1998, 3.

tion, in July 1993, of establishing a confederation of three ethno-national states—Serbian, Croatian, and Muslim—in Bosnia-Herzegovina. This suggestion meant the end of the existing international recognition of Bosnia-Herzegovina as a state.[8] It inspired the Owen-Stoltenberg plan for peace in Bosnia-Herzegovina, presented at the peace talks held in Geneva at the end of July 1993.

This carving-up of Bosnia-Herzegovina into three ethnic parts accorded perfectly with three demands. It met the demand of Milošević and Tuđman that achieving their goal of two unified Serbian and Croatian ethno-national states would be possible only by dividing Bosnia-Herzegovina, as justified by the irreconcilable tensions and hatreds inside the latter country. It fulfilled any Muslim desires for a "safe" mini-state. So whose was the third demand?

The war was started by the neighbors of Bosnia-Herzegovina and supported and guided by their ethno-national power groups. It now demanded an urgent peace solution, which, like any such solution, would be based on reaching a compromise between all sides in the conflict. The war itself was seen as evidence that the anti-Bosnian theories of ancient hatreds and bloodlusts, which could be stopped only by dividing the peoples into separate ethno-national territories, were correct. Preserving Bosnia-Herzegovina's unity, including a mixed society of Bosniaks, Serbs, and Croats throughout her territory, would require, according to this interpretation, the lasting presence of foreign military forces and a huge financial outlay.

The "divide and quit" theory, which the British had already propounded with regard to the conflicts between Hindus and Muslims in India, Jews and Arabs in Palestine, Greeks and Turks in Cyprus, and Catholics and Protestants in Ireland, appeared to be the most appropriate response to the events in Bosnia-Herzegovina. This theory was promoted and accepted from the beginning of the peace efforts in Bosnia-Herzegovina: first by Peter Carrington, and after him by David Owen. Bosnia-Herzegovina was judged to be a "historical accident" in which, according to Ćosić, "Bosniaks, Croats, and Serbs cannot and will not live together any longer"[9] and which should be divided up.

Such judgments—the "artificiality" of Bosnia-Herzegovina, "clash of civilizations," "sinister" Muslim intentions, geopolitical necessity, "historical right," and so on—led to an ever-greater denial, weakening, and splitting of Bosnia-Herzegovina's unity and statehood. The war that Serbia and Croatia

8. For details of this proposal, produced in cooperation with D. Owen on 9 July 1993 in Zagreb, see K. I. Begić's book, *Bosna i Hercegovina od Vanceove misije do Daytonskog sporazuma* [Bosnia and Herzegovina from the Vance mission to the Dayton agreement] (Sarajevo, 1997).

9. See Chapter 10 note 3.

had launched against Bosnia-Herzegovina was reduced to an "internal conflict," which could be interpreted however one wished: civil, religious, or whatever. It seems that this distortion of the Bosnian-Herzegovinan drama actually contributed to the validation of Huntington's ideological matrix as a model for understanding and solving conflicts throughout the world.

It is unsurprising, therefore, that Jadranko Prlić (Bosnia's Foreign Affairs Minister at the time of writing) tried to connect the division of Bosnia with Huntington's theory. Prlić claimed that the Serbs in Bosnia were tending toward a "pan-Orthodox pluralism" and "had removed themselves from the European system of values." Meanwhile, the Bosniaks "have not completely succeeded in rejecting the call of Islamic civilization" and have "accepted re-Islamification and the rejection of a non-Islamic identity. . . . The smallest change in identity was suffered by the Bosnian Croats, who have shown their loyalty to European civilization."[10] This statement is completely in accord with the Croatian plan for justifying the division of Bosnia-Herzegovina. For Tuđman, all events in Bosnia "have a deep historical, religious, national, ethnic, and, what is more, cultural incompatibility." In this region, he remarks, "political acts define themselves in terms of different civilizations."[11]

This model is founded on the premise that current and future relations in the world are and will be defined by the territories of separate civilization, with those that align themselves in opposition to Western liberal democracy (Confucian China and Islamic Iran) confronting those defined by unions such as NATO or the European community.

Civilizations define themselves by their links with individual cultural entities, different in "meaning, symbols, values, and ideas," and religious and ideological distinctions are the result. (This might suggest that all "civilizations" have the potential to realize the basic unity of their sacred roots, and thus are capable of transcending all historical manifestations—but Huntington ignores this possibility in his model, thus making it a fundamentally atheistic one.) This type of model "for interpreting the geopolitical events of the current world," as Huntington calls it, finds particular favor in those contemporary "intellectual" circles defined by historical ignorance and prejudice, which specialize in hating the Other. The Islamophobic obsessions of a great number of intellectuals seem *a priori* acceptable to Huntington's model, which can be used to support all forms of political and ideological exclusivity.

10. From a speech by Jadranko Prlić at the conference *Bosnia and Herzegovina after Dayton,* held in March 1997 in Zagreb, as quoted by *Oslobođenje,* 18 March 1997, 3.

11. F. Tuđman, in an interview with leading Croatian media editors, published in *Vjesnik* (Zagreb), 13 September 1997, 3.

This explains why those who employ Huntington's model for interpreting the war against Bosnia are so numerous. They claim that this war was a classic example of the "conflict of civilizations." Tuđman finds in it theoretical support for his all-embracing anti-Bosnianism. "According to this, it could be concluded," he says,

> that, in the region of Bosnia and Herzegovina, the policy of those international circles which would like a unitary multi-ethnic, multicultural Bosnia clashes with that of those who accept the reality that—as many representatives of American political and intellectual life, such as Kissinger and Huntington, have said—the modern world is composed of incompatible civilizations, and that these opposites are today revealing themselves plainly on the ground in Bosnia-Herzegovina, and that they should be taken into account. [12]

Although Huntington can hardly be accused of having the same goals as Milošević and Tuđman, his model showed that the latter could point to the conflicts they themselves had incited within Bosnia as evidence of incompatibility of civilizations and thus gain support for their Greater Serbian and Greater Croatian plans. This explains their paradoxical treatment of Muslim ethnonational policy: pushing it forward with one hand and pointing to it in horror with the other. The model incorporates a double method of interpreting world events, both parts of which gave the anti-Bosnian designs of Milošević and Tuđman a seemingly sound theoretical basis and political conviction.

The first part of the interpretation starts by defining areas of Orthodox civilization on the premise that they have shown themselves, on the stage of world politics and culture, to be the unstable and retrogressive base of the Communist-Stalinist empire. It follows that liberal democracy, the precondition for modernization, can only have a hypothetical future in this part of the world. The fall of the Communist empire, which was for the most part one of the Orthodox world, showed that this world is incapable of superseding the world of Western-style liberal democracy and market forces. Therefore it must itself undergo reform in the direction of liberal democracy and free market conditions. A significant part in this process can be played by the Christian basis underlying both worlds. Thus Milošević and Tuđman, whose names can be taken as symbolizing the dual objectives of the anti-Bosnian plan, are justified in their search for "a total solution for the Serbian and Croatian nations as a whole."

12. Tuđman interview, *Vjesnik,* 13 September 1997.

In the second part of the interpretation, the nature of the ruling systems and the status of human rights in all those countries where Muslims live are identified with, and ascribed to, Islamic teaching and tradition. This provides clear support for the political and ideological strategies that aim to destroy Bosnia. The history of the Bosniaks, the heirs of Islam, has in recent centuries been one of a lengthy battle for survival, a repeated succession of utopian expectations on the one hand, and killings and persecutions on the other.[13] No unified political plan has ever been formed to enable this people to contest all the challenges made against the evidence of its historical and cultural right to nationhood. There is no systematic understanding of the nature of anti-Muslim ideology in their immediate and wider vicinity. Therefore, they are vulnerable to political forces such as the manipulation of sacred tradition and its exploitation for ideological purposes. The anti-Bosnian plan relied on this vulnerability. The Bosniaks were encouraged with all means at hand to embrace a "Muslim" state instead of that of Bosnia-Herzegovina. Simultaneously, they were accused of harboring precisely this desire. Therefore—and of this there can no longer be any doubt—those individuals and groups among the Bosniaks who favored "Islamicization" received encouragement and support, and those who persisted in the defense of Bosnian unity were marginalized and denied.

Thus the course of Bosnian events was reduced to a simplistic picture, of a kind unacceptable to the prevailing intellectual and political modes of thought in the West. This had the side effect of suppressing awareness of the most important dynamics of international conflict, that is, the effect of politico-ideological factors, of which the war in Bosnia was a genuine manifestation.

The simplistic nature of the "conflict of civilizations" theory is destructive not only for Bosnia and its people, but also in terms of perceiving the totality of world events. It denies or simplifies the present and future nature of cultural and political pluralism in the world.[14] For if the "conflict of civilizations" the-

13. In the last two decades of the nineteenth century and the first two decades of the twentieth, this people lost, by resettlement, more than a third of their demographic presence in the country. By genocide and other causes in the Second World War this people suffered the greatest proportion of killings after the Bosnian Jews (9 percent of the total population). In the period from 1991 to 1995, around 160,000 Bosniaks (8 percent) were killed, and a further 500,000 or more (26 percent) became refugees. In the last three centuries, the territory on which they once lived has been reduced by 90 percent. After the 1991–95 war, the amount of Bosnian-Herzegovinan territory on which they lived was reduced from 95 percent to around 22 percent. These figures show this people to be significantly endangered. Their survival is uncertain—unless vital changes in their environment and in themselves take place.

14. Every logical model imposed on reality ends up contradicting itself. Failure to understand this can have serious consequences, as can be seen in Jadranko Prlić's thesis. The horrific consequences of the anti-Bosnian policy of the Croatian ethno-national leadership culminated in the systematic destruction o the Muslim presence in Stolac, Čapljina, Prozor, Mostar, and other zones under Croatian military control and the establishment of concentration camps for more than twenty thousand Bosniaks. On 15 January

ory is valid for Bosnia, then it can equally be applied to the Holocaust, which took place here among us, in the heart of Europe, not five centuries but just five decades ago. If this theory can provide a justification for the campaign against Bosnia, as the campaign's advocates maintain, then it is worth noting that it can be employed to do the same for the Holocaust. The reality that this model is a theoretical conceit, though it appeals to the prevailing mentality, is clear from the obvious impossibility of explaining away the numerous other conflicts of Europe as "conflicts of civilizations." For the Basque struggle and the Irish conflict, which are only a couple of ongoing examples, are far from being "conflicts of civilizations." Huntington's model is as incapable of explaining them as it is of explaining the Holocaust.

Huntington's model is, in fact, a naïve if not sinister attempt to interpret world events on the basis of a triumphalist, not to say imperialist, perception of Western values. These are seen not as part of the rich multiplicity of world ideas, but as the ultimate human achievement, which must prevail—even at the price of war. This excuses every kind of political and other prejudice but is powerless to explain the complexity of the world. The sacred nuclei of "civilizations" are perceived as mutually opposed, and therefore the cultures that spring from these nuclei must necessarily be in conflict. The alternate view—that such conflict means a betrayal and a denial of the true nature of these nuclei—is ignored. The faithful believers in Huntington's model are either ignorant about the foundations of their cultural individuality or deliberately choose to ignore them.

The "conflict of civilizations" theory is inseparable from the influence of sectarianism as the basis of contemporary national ideology. If religious systems are isolated from their transcendent, unifying potential, the result is oversimplification, self-righteousness, and cruelty. The core elements of religion can be seen as transcending divisions and conflicts. They declare, first and foremost, that every man must strive toward perfection and that external differences in means can be dismissed as secondary. But this interpretation is not recognized or accepted by the majority who remain bound up in their sects and

---

1997, the International War Crimes Tribunal for the Former Yugoslavia in the Hague ordered twenty-seven officers of the Croatian army serving in Bosnia to appear before it by means of a subpoena sent to the Republic of Croatia and its Defense Minister Gojko Šušak, and published in the Zagreb daily *Nacional* of 13 August 1997. Jadranko Prlić, president of the Croatian Republic of Herceg-Bosna at the time when these crimes were committed and an alliance was being engineered with the "Republika Srpska" (which was supported on the eve of its proclamation by F. Tudman), says: "Regarding Croatian policy in Bosnia-Herzegovina we can say what we wish, but this is a policy that 95 percent of Croats in Bosnia-Herzegovina supported. And if Croatian policy in Bosnia is under accusation, then the Croatian people in Bosnia-Herzegovina are also being accused" (quote from an interview with Prlić, *Nacional,* 13 August 1997, 63).

cliques. Alienated from the Center, they quarrel about names. They deny the human right to perfection and put the rule of ideologies in its place. Civilizations can conflict, it is true, but only when they are separated from that source without which they are worth nothing and without which they represent only a multitude of dead forms. In the same way, the most frequent contemporary usage of the term "civilization" has lost its ancient value. [15]

The destruction of the foundations of and conditions for a pluralist society in Bosnia is in fundamental opposition to the highest principles of Western culture. The survival of ethno-national, religious, cultural, and political multiplicity depends on forces that inspire trust—and trust in its origin and achievements must always be deeper and wider than a simplistic social contract based on a rationalization of human nature and needs. The justification of any crime by appealing to the principles of Western civilization or Christianity is a crime against both. If civilization is a higher-order social structure characterized by the advance of knowledge, art, and so on, then it is clearly possible to claim that in Bosnia there were differences of "civilization" between Croats, Serbs, and Bosniaks. The chief—in fact, just about the only—difference was a difference of religion: Catholicism, Orthodoxy, and Islam. The real story, therefore, might be called one of the conflict of religions. But this would deny the essence of the sacred foundations of all three religions. It follows that this conflict is, in fact, a political betrayal of religion.

Bosnia's being is built on the immutable foundations of religions and civilizations, of a world with a future. If this being can be destroyed in Bosnia or anywhere else, this is an ill omen for the future of the world. The war against Bosnia was a planned criminal enterprise. The puppet-masters and executors of this campaign viewed it much as did the authors of the "final solution" to the Jewish question. But the nature of truth is such that it is rarely without its advocates for long, and they are ultimately, it is hoped, stronger and more dedicated than the advocates of crime.

The forces working against Bosnia, therefore, are not rooted in religion or civilization, but in ideology, by which all human relationships with divine Intellect are forced into the straitjacket of nationalist plans or repudiated if they offer resistance. The destruction of Bosnia and the four years of slaughter are proof that the connection of individuals and groups with the Center has been lost. Reverence and wonder were left powerless when assaulted by systems constructed to satisfy egoistic human needs for material gain and power over the world and over all within it.

15. See, for example, A. K. Coomaraswamy, *What Is Civilization?* (Cambridge, 1989).

Disintegration and destruction have been and still are central to all thinking about Bosnia. Nor has the Bosniak political leadership reacted in a way likely to defeat the products of such thinking. It is not merely a case of the absence of a unified and comprehensive analysis of what the anti-Bosniak plans actually entailed. By dropping the principle of Bosnia-Herzegovina's unity and accepting "their own role," the Bosniak leadership significantly weakened their own position. Bosnia-Herzegovina is only possible as a joint enterprise involving all her people, whether they define themselves as Bosniaks, Croats, Gypsies, Jews, Serbs, or others. Her unity can survive and become sustainable only if the interconnections between all her peoples are broadened and strengthened. Narrowing the scope of the union only reduces the likelihood of preserving Bosnia's unity. Nor is the Bosniak political leadership guiltless with regard to a series of episodes that effectively weakened the union to defend Bosnia and her statehood. These include the absence of any convincing and coherent multi-ethnic political strategy; the attempts to replace one ideology in the education system with another; the open linkage of religion to politics; the failure to ensure rights for all peoples in the areas of accommodation, employment, education, and so on; the lack of transparency in use of public funds, opening the way to discriminatory abuse of funding; a blatant lack of sensitivity, in choosing street names, for example, and many other failures.

The claim that Bosniak resistance to destructive political pressures was inadequate requires additional explanation. The war against Bosnia and Herzegovina left the Bosniaks with very little choice. The only alternative to defense was surrender. But the suicidal option of surrender was seen by some as salvation. As the war went on, complex and cunning pressures were exerted during political negotiations. In the face of the policies that united Greater Serbia and Greater Croatia, Bosniak policy became separated, or was forced to become separated, from Bosnian-Herzegovinan unity. In the majority of peace talks, the forces were physically aligned so that the Bosniak negotiators were frequently isolated on one side of the negotiating table and the representatives of Greater Serbia, Greater Croatia, and, very often, the representatives of the international community, were ranged on the other side. These pressures also took the form of concealing or disguising the nature of the war, the killing, and the destruction. The primacy of justice was denied, and policies of "tea and sympathy," "holding onto what we can," and "saving the Bosniak nation from total destruction" were adopted in its place. This also ignored the fact that the Bosniak people, aided by those Serbs and Croats who remained Bosnian in outlook, did actually succeed, although at a horrific cost, in defending themselves. This proof that Bosnia could be saved should have been used to give more room for Bosnianism as an association of all peoples; however, the peace proposals only had the effect of narrowing this space and hardening division.

The peace solution that was finally produced was based on the "conflict of civilizations" uniting "different worlds" to form a strange postwar monster: a model of destruction that was expected to become one of construction. This short-sighted model of human conflict, which met its *reductio ad absurdum* in the war against Bosnia, was blind to the fact that the chief goal of the war was, quite simply, the destruction of Bosnia. Nevertheless, powerful though it may be, it is only one of many ideological interpretations of the destruction of Bosnia-Herzegovina, some of them more helpful, some less. But what we lack is a proper model for reconstructing and rebuilding Bosnia.

The goal of peace should be the exact opposite of the goal of war: building up a viable state on the basis of good will and trust between all its members.

15

BUILDING A NUCLEUS

The reconstruction of Bosnia is centered on efforts to establish and develop political structures in two violently and artificially separated parts of the state and the facilitation of joint political action through a joint presidency, two houses of parliament, a council of ministers, a constitutional court, and a stock exchange. The whole undertaking is supervised, guided, and coordinated by the Office of the High Representative, who acts as an overseer with significant power in his own right. This is the framework for the long-overdue reform of all the political and economic bodies dating from the Communist era, which were transformed in the war into separate entities, each with a military, police, or financial power base, but with no legally defined interlinkage between them.

The structuring and development of the economy is understood to be the key framework around which Bosnian unity must grow and sustain itself. This model is possible in the current circumstances only with the presence of institutions and organizations of the international community, backed up by NATO and the international policing force. But it is more than evident that the model omits or ignores two important elements, which must be addressed if the framework is not to collapse.

At the root of economic development (that is, the type of development that is synonymous with liberal democracy and a free-market economy) lies a scientific method that enables action to be taken through empirical observation and experience. This method requires an understanding of the higher levels of causation through the interaction of abstract ideas with physical principles. However, this is not a self-sustaining process; it needs to be rooted in traditional culture. The ideological exploitation of economics, however, reduced to three ethno-national plans, will not only prevent economic stability but will be the source of future conflicts and divisions.

Therefore it is vital to ascertain the following: is there a transnational Bosnian community that can develop in order to represent an intellectual force capable of reconciling individual goals? Such a community is not only the precondition for rooting the sapling of economic growth in Bosnia-Herzegovina, it is the pre-condition for preserving the living nucleus of Bosnia's individuality. Under the Communist system, all evidence of community was used to deny individuality. Liberalism is, as is known, historically derived from the campaign to keep religion out of the direct or indirect management of the state. But few theoreticians of liberalism consider that religions should actually be excluded from society itself. In today's Bosnia, all efforts to guide economic reconstruction that are founded on the principle of rationalizing desires and actions in order to achieve the greatest material gain will be fruitless if they do not include a clear and acceptable relationship toward Bosnia's religious traditions, in other words, toward the bedrock of Bosnian culture. Three distinct ethno-national entities are present in the Bosnia of today. This is the consequence of the development of a multireligious population during the course of the last two centuries. Bearing in mind the international recognition of the Bosnian-Herzegovinan state, it can be claimed that this country has developed under conditions significantly different from any other in Europe.

In one state three ethno-national individualities exist side by side, but there is no agreement between them over the constitution of the state itself. One can say, therefore, that there is no distinct state consciousness. But without this, it is difficult to foresee the survival of the state itself. Therefore, the development of such a consciousness is the key question for Bosnia-Herzegovina's future. If reconstruction is confined within the ideological limits of the Communist inheritance and its ethno-nationalistic reaction, there is very little likelihood of such a consciousness developing. Most contemporary European states developed more or less in tune with the development of an ethno-national consciousness, while the modern Bosnian-Herzegovinan state sprang up before the ethno-national entities within it had reached any sort of agreement. Such an agreement must be the main goal of all future action in the political, economic, and cultural spheres.

However, for a long time the state will be torn between two opposite pressures: one internal, which will demand agreement as vital to all peoples of Bosnia-Herzegovina, and one external, which will deny, prevent, and destroy agreement for the sake of hegemonist and imperialist goals. The most significant external sources of pressure will remain the designs for a Greater Croatia and Greater Serbia, channeled through various intermediaries. Internal pressure toward agreement can result in a viable state that is a member of the international community and open to geopolitical trends, while external pressure can only oppose this tendency.

If dialogue between those of different religious outlooks is crucial in the world at large, then creating and managing such a dialogue in Bosnia can form a pattern for action throughout the world. Such dialogue cannot recommence without widespread understanding and support. But Bosnia has no future if no intellectual and organizational framework is constructed for such a dialogue, for the 80 percent solution that the economy offers cannot ensure either peace or renewal while the status quo prevails. Explaining and resolving the Bosnian enigma on the basis of an economic model is necessary, but not sufficient. Therefore, recognizing the individuality of all elements in the Bosnian tapestry and their connection to one and the same source is the precondition for trust and dialogue. This will enable the establishment of a multi-ethnic Bosnian community, within which all individuals and groups can live their lives to the fullest, according to the principle of "our God and your God are one and the same God."

Thus, in essence, establishing Bosnia's unity means understanding and developing her separate elements, in their full human potential for goodness and beauty and the rejection of evil. The cruelty of sectarianism and factionalism will be transformed if the life of every man is seen once more as sacred and wonderful. But the development of social capital within each of Bosnia's elements is possible only through mutual interaction. This capital cannot be amassed or sustained within a merely economic frame. Liberal democracy can transcend current separatism only if it is realized that for one culture to use just its own scale of values in evaluating another culture is a way of imposing its own meanings, symbols, and ideas on others.

We have accepted for the purposes of this essay that the course of human history is defined by the interaction between the selfish human need to obtain and secure the greatest gains possible, on the one hand, and the need for every individual and community to be recognized as what they feel themselves to be, on the other. Therefore, the destruction of Bosnian unity can be ascribed not only to the negative power of the first need but also to the failure to recognize and meet the second. Any resolution of the Bosnia-Herzegovina problem will have to address the first, although the second has the greater destructive potential. The need for recognition, whether on an individual or a group level, must be met by establishing conditions for permanent dialogue between those who need acknowledgment from each other. Opposing separatism by dialogue, with the rejection of all forms of ideology that endanger the principle of human equality, will enable contact with a common center and call a halt to division and conflict.

"Concerning the neoclassical economy we can think of it as eighty percent exact. But there is a missing twenty percent of human behavior about which neoclassical economics can give only a poor account. As Adam Smith well understood, economic life is deeply embedded in social life, and it cannot be understood in isolation from the customs, morals, and habits of the society in which it occurs. In short, it cannot be divorced from culture. Consequently, we have been ill served by contemporary debates that fail to take account of these cultural factors."[1] But if, for economic development, a comprehensive understanding of human greed is 80 percent of the total and the participation of culture only 20 percent, then the reverse is probably true for campaigns of destruction. In the ideologically-led campaign against Bosnia, culture was responsible for up to 80 percent, and rational concepts of the goals of the destruction comprised only 20 percent. Overcoming the sources of this destruction, therefore, requires a more precise evaluation of the culture of those who shared in Bosnia's unity and in its destruction.

Post-Dayton events in Bosnia-Herzegovina are still defined by the consequences of war aims—the original anti-Bosnian plans of the Greater Serbian and Greater Croatian ethno-national elites and the behavior of the Bosniak ethno-national elite, which began as a reaction but gradually turned into their mirror-image. These elites established and preserved power over the areas that were captured and "consolidated" by the three armies. But not one of the sides believes that the Dayton Agreement produced a situation acceptable from the standpoint of their original desires.

The disintegration of Bosnia-Herzegovina's unity goes hand in hand with a process of accretion around ethnic nuclei that refuse to countenance any linkage with any other nucleus within Bosnia. They are opposed to any vision of Bosnian-Herzegovinan unity that would involve the linking up of all her elements. The Serbian and the Croatian nuclei look for support outside Bosnia, in their respective ethno-national power centers. The Bosniak side, tied inevitably to Bosnia-Herzegovina herself but defined as "Muslim," cannot escape the fact that any efforts to establish and strengthen their country's unity

1. F. Fukuyama, *Trust: The Social Virtues and the Creation of Prosperity* (London, 1995), 13.

are seen as justifying Croatian and Serbian efforts against Bosnia-Herzegovina. Thus the nucleus round which it would be possible for the elements of a Bosnian-Herzegovinan unity to gather remains rudimentary. And it will remain so, given the prevailing political climate: the leaders of "Srpska" and "Herceg-Bosna" are prepared to accept only as much of a joint state constitution and executive bodies as do not seem to endanger their "sovereignty" in the areas that they perceive as exclusively "theirs."

The result is fertile ground only for organized crime, illegal cash-flows, and the continued operation of organizations outside the rule of law. Simultaneously, all these networks and organizations only harden the ethno-national structure established in the form of sectarian parastates on the divided parts of Bosnia-Herzegovina's territory.

The Dayton Agreement foresaw the organized presence of the international community as a guarantee for the acceptance of the peace package. This presence puts most of its efforts into preventing military conflict, establishing political institutions and organizations defined by the Agreement, and creating the political preconditions for economic renewal and growth. In the approach to democratic elections for these institutions and organizations within the legal state framework, the same forces that entered onto the political stage shortly before the war and dominated it during the war are again taking the lead. Their political thinking is defined above all by Communist ideology and the power system that sprang from it, although they present themselves as anti-Communist, antidogmatic, and prodemocratic.

Such thought patterns cannot be changed overnight, which is the main reason why issues of the Bosnian-Herzegovinan state are being tackled on the basis of logical models in which political organizations are given equivalent value to government. In parallel with this, there is a tendency to identify political organizations with ethno-national groups and with ethno-religious communities. In such circumstances, intellectual communities labor, in accordance with habits acquired under the previous system, to get the support and protection of their "own" ethno-national parties and ethno-religious communities. Any opposition to this mentality meets with fierce resistance, which discourages critical thinking and any movement toward change.

The complex implications of the Dayton Agreement, entailing a multitude of compromises in relation to the Bosnian-Herzegovinan state, mean that little attention has been paid to the question of intellectual reunification. The reduction of the sum of social action to politics continues to be a substitute for action in the social arena. Therefore, the establishment of new intellectual networks, above all in culture and art, is a precondition for weakening the existing emphasis on ethno-political organizations.

16

Acquiring and securing material wealth, and the need for recognition, are two basic human requirements. While the first could be fulfilled by efficient organizations of education and employment, the other is significantly more deeply rooted in nature, and its requirements more complex and more difficult to satisfy. Although the first element, being external, can be catered to by a rational plan, it is closely connected with the other, which appears in the symbols, meanings and interpretations that define the nature of every civilization. This second element belongs to the realm of Mind or Intellect in one of its oldest senses: that of the supra-individual.

Social efficiency, as defined by the rational principle of the greatest utility, is based on the human capacity for association. Therefore, it can be claimed that the capacity for such association, and its development in accordance with set goals, depends to a large extent on people's inner connections with the supra-individual archetypes of symbol and meaning—in other words, on the capacity to recognize, within a culture, reasons to put one's trust in others who are part of the same community or society. Although these religious symbols all point toward union with the transcendent center or source, religious communities gain strength and resilience largely by uniting their members through symbols and language as the foundations of a common culture. This community, once established, can use these symbols for constructive or destructive purposes. These involve establishing a certain rational plan, whose roots always lie outside the area of the plan itself.

The war against Bosnia was based on a systematically-developed, rational plan. But its roots lay significantly deeper, in the symbols and meanings through which a rationalized "national feeling" was developed. It is of decisive importance, accordingly, to identify these deeper roots. If this plan is defined simply as establishing, for example, Serbian ethno-national government over those areas that Serbs share with others, with the goal that this state be totally "Serbian," then all others who live in those same areas are an obstacle to this plan. They must be removed so that the territory can be declared free for "nation-building." The undertaking must be rationalized within the context of the specific place and time. National consciousness must be transformed in such a way that the whole of the history of the "nation" testifies to the right of the builders to destroy the obstacle. Such a model of history has to be linked to the will of God Himself. The Others, since they oppose the plan, are opposing God himself, as they have done throughout history. The Muslim Slavs, hardly different in language and identical in ethnic origin, but having allegedly spurned the communal roots, must be comprehensively portrayed throughout their history as the alien, the enemy.

There is also the fact that Muslims are not living just on the margins of Serbian-inhabited lands, nor on the periphery of Serbian history, but right in the middle of it, organically inside it. While other relationships are more clearly defined and borders exist between them independent of the strength of one side or the other, borders with the Muslims are impossible to draw. They are part of the internal situation on which the strength of the ethno-national plan depends. Therefore, when raising people's consciousness of their right to have a national state and the way in which this can be done, it is necessary to raise awareness about the right to eradicate the Muslim presence and the ways in which this can be done. This is characteristic of the ethno-national plan. The strength of mutual trust advertised by the national plan is equaled by the mistrust of Muslims. Muslim persistence in justifying and defending the concept of coexistence is dangerous, and rejection of and resistance to it must be absolute. And Muslims too must be taught to participate in the general distrust.

Appealing to religious origins gives support to the ethno-national plan, enabling it to include every individual and the very essence of nationhood and, on a wider basis, win the sympathy and support of those who are familiar with the same religious symbols and meanings. God is no longer the God of all worlds, nor just, nor merciful. In the ideologized consciousness He is reduced to an idol created in the likeness of the ethno-national models.

Such a model cannot, however, achieve fulfillment for long, for it will always be opposed by that part of individual and group consciousness that cannot ignore human responsibilities, nor accept that humanity should be left without a transcendent, unifying element. It will oppose this division with the creative force that contributes to the origins of human nature, by which differences are only a sign of accord and different roads always wind toward one and the same center. This multiple concept of trust has been visible throughout the history of Bosnia. Different religious teachings have coexisted for a thousand years. The multiple presence of these different concepts has demonstrated the right of individuals and communities to choose their own road and way of life, with these choices always being seen as relative, since each choice is an individual interpretation and never the whole or only truth. The different choices all contain the possibility of reaching the Center, which is always one and the same and through which every human individual is a reflection of and a potential part of the Absolute.

This is the nucleus of the Bosnian plan of trust, as opposed to the national plans and their nationalized gods. Simply showing trust is much closer to the center of humanity than any external action, whether this action is promoted by the desire to do good to others or merely hopes to achieve the greatest possible gain. Trust testifies to those parts of human nature that turn toward perfection, and away from evil.

The fact that trust was deliberately sabotaged is demonstrated by a series of examples taken from publicly accessible sources, showing how the anti-Bosnian conspiracies refuted any evidence of the existence of trust and emphasized and, where necessary, invented the opposite: hatred, killings, falsehoods, atrocities, and the like. The whole history of Bosnia-Herzegovina is interpreted against this remorseless backdrop of ugliness and evil. This picture was painted to facilitate division, so that the envisioned ethno-national areas could be achieved more easily by way of the resulting spiritual divide. The denial and destruction of trust between the elements in Bosnia-Herzegovina's unity was the first step in the plan. In such an interpretation, hatred, killing, and expulsion are needed by the destroyers. This enables them to champion "peaceful dissolution," that is, separating the antagonists in order to prevent conflict.

This model was much more visible in war than in peace. In war, the complex whole of the anti-Bosnia-Herzegovina plan was crystalized into a number of smaller elements that were both more savage and more obvious. Slowly, the intentions behind the trickery grew more plain.

Remembering the long hardship of the war enables one to understand other, equally savage currents otherwise hidden behind the skillful ploys that established the armistice. The same participants remain in power. Their goals unachieved or partially achieved, they interpreted the peace proposals as victory and started producing a new history, in which they reverse the positions of criminals and victims, attack and defense, destroying and building. Only the rediscovery of trust, and the ways of strengthening it, will enable the formation of an intellectual community powerful enough to challenge these destructive histories and address the manifestations they have produced in social life. This is one of the best chances for the future of the country whose destiny is being discussed in this essay.

If the defense of Bosnia-Herzegovina is reduced to the defense of ethnically-held regions "frozen" by armistice as a sign of the unfinished work of disintegration, the existing division between the Federation and the Republika Srpska will be understood as a temporary situation, a step on the way to the final goal of territorial division between Serbia and Croatia. As Franjo Tuđman declared in 1991, "If the demand of Serbia that all Serbs live in one state is taken seriously, then nobody can deny the same right to the Croats."[1]

It follows that the disintegration of trust between the two current halves of Bosnia-Herzegovina, the Federation and the Republika Srpska, must be continued in order to achieve the goals for which the war was started by Bosnia-Herzegovina's neighbors. Without strong foundations of trust, there is little chance that these goals can be successfully opposed. The whole country is now *de jure* divided into two (*de facto* into three) areas of interest, all of which declare themselves to be valid participants in the geopolitical formation of Europe. Serbia's presence in Srpska continues to be active, and the influence of Croatia is blatant in parts of the Federation.

Preventing these parts from splitting away completely depends on the commitment of individuals and groups to this torn and exhausted state. The life of Bosnia has been frozen and paralyzed by recent events, far more than even the Second World War managed to do. Bosnia's current state has been faithfully portrayed by H. Kohn: "Twentieth-century man has become less confident than his nineteenth-century ancestor was. He has witnessed the dark powers of history in his own experience. Things which seemed to belong to the past have reappeared: fanatical faith, infallible leaders, slavery and massacres, the uprooting of whole populations, ruthlessness and barbarism."[2]

This situation of fear and disintegration is most applicable to Bosnia today. To overcome it, both hard effort and help will be necessary, based on exploring existing opportunities and challenging and overcoming deep-rooted prejudices.

1. Quoted in Judah, "Creation of Islamic Buffer State"; see also Chapter 10 note 9.
2. H. Kohn, *The Twentieth Century* (New York, 1949), 53.

17

TWO RENEWALS

The mutilation of Bosnia shows itself in the fragmentation of all trade connections between residential and economic areas. This has established internal borders, which have tried hard and are still trying, to become the borders of neighboring states. The lines of division between A and H areas [1] are intended, in a political, military, trade, and industrial sense, to become the borders defining the Croatian state and its ethno-national sovereignty, while the borders between A and S are intended to define the Serbian state and its ethno-national sovereignty. All remaining forms of state and ethno-national sovereignty between these two areas should be presented as historically in need of the permanent guardianship allegedly necessary for the "Europeanizing" of the Muslims. Any reasons for Bosnia-Herzegovina to be a unified state must be suppressed because of the dangers inherent in an irreconcilable "conflict of civilizations."

Two reasons are offered most frequently in attempts to justify the splitting of Bosnia, the first rationalist and the second cultural. Serbian ethno-national unity, which is supported by Serbian cultural unity, can only be established, according to this plan, in a unified political, economic, and cultural space. This

---

1. Area A is the part of Bosnia-Herzegovina territory under the control of the Army of Bosnia-Herzegovina (around 22 percent); area H is the part under control of the Croatian Military Council (HVO) (around 29 percent); area S is under control of the Republika Srpska Army (around 49 percent).

also holds true for the Croatian economy and Croatian ethno-national unity. But this is incompatible with Bosnia-Herzegovina's unity, which demonstrates the impossibility of ethnic, cultural, economic, and political redefinition without the use of force. Establishing ethno-national states is possible only by splitting Bosnia-Herzegovina. This has to involve various types of force. The first task is to disentangle the demographic complex, which is possible only by genocidally removing the Other. All cultural elements which cannot be slotted into an ideologized consciousness of Us and Them must be destroyed or discarded. Next, new political and economic entities must be created. But were this plan to be tested in the light of contemporary economic theories, it would be clear that the economic reasons for reestablishing Bosnian unity supersede the mostly irrational motives for dividing the country.

Economic behavior is essentially founded in social life and cannot be understood in isolation from the customs and mores of the society involved. This means that economic behavior cannot be divided from culture. When the reasons for Bosnian unity are examined, it is possible, without especial difficulty, to find a number of economic justifications. But these reasons usually reflect the nature of the environment and the diversity of the culture in their complexity. Those elements that are not purely economic—political, bureaucratic, nationalist, and others—should be given greater attention than is currently the case in any attempts to analyze the divisive factors in Bosnia.

While it is true that people are largely motivated by selfish goals, their behavior cannot be reduced just to the question of rational utility. But however greatly tradition influences behavior, a rational component can always be found. Thus, although the expulsion and killing of Muslims is linked to irrational perceptions, the territories taken by genocide provide lebensraum as well as loot.

The plans for ethnic nation-states rely on ethno-national trust in order to fulfill the ruling elite's ideological goals. But the ethics on which this trust is based are themselves deformed, a fact that must ultimately produce hidden internal conflicts. The ethics of nationalism are incapable of establishing a society and state in which a community can live and act in accord with general ethical rules. Any trust created inside ethno-national communities that is chiefly a reflection of the artificial distrust of everybody outside the community will survive as long as the genocidal plan is operational. But the trust that is needed for the community to become a full society cannot be established if the community is based on values solely from the past, unless an additional twisting of history firmly teaches its readers where to put the blame. But this, in turn, produces a mutilated individual and social consciousness, preventing the establishment of trust (defined here as a group expectation of legal, honest, and cooperative behavior, springing from a common tradition).

This form of social capital develops from the prevalence of trust among the members of the society. It differs from all other forms of capital in being inextricably bound up with the slow course of social development. A social contract can supersede it. But the effectiveness and reliability of that contract will always be limited by the strength of inherited trust. A contract alone, without trust, cannot regulate the relationships between individuals and parts of society. Amassing this type of capital depends on the readiness of prevailing social norms to change. Put differently, this social capital cannot be produced by decisions taken at an individual level, however high that level may be. It is founded on the strength of social rather than individual virtues.

Efficient economic development requires trust, regardless of differences. But this poses a question: how precisely do economic efficiency and trust relate to each other? Starting from the premise that humanity is created to work toward perfection, we can claim that nobody is allowed to ignore the demands on behavior posed by human virtues. One of their chief demands is that the individual should display goodness toward his or her neighbor. Powerful as this demand is, it always has the potential to grow stronger. It depends to some extent on social and cultural environment, but it can never be totally ignored. If a society is economically efficient at all levels, this is due to the ethos of care for others, transformed into trust between organized groups. This efficiency can never be wholly based on utilitarian reasoning. The narrow and selfish energies of individuals organized within ethno-national plans are used up in the pursuit of the goals set by the plan. After the conflict, these destructive groups are left in a vacuum. Their presence must inevitably be superseded by a committed campaign on the part of those who believe that social development is possible by accepting and strengthening trust. In particular, this means the trust that enables social institutions and economic contracts to be formed as preconditions for normal life.

Building trust rests on cultural foundations. Any productive or economic system is indivisibly connected with culture. Looking at the differences of culture and the social establishment, it is possible to say that culture is defined by symbols, values, and ideas: it covers phenomena like religion and ideology. Culture is the historical process of interpreting and developing the meanings embodied in symbols: a system of inherited thought, expressed in symbols, develops the knowledge of and shapes attitudes toward life. Culture is not a rational choice, unlike economic behavior, which can often be proved, in spite of its cultural content, to have a rational base. Although the process of confirming and maintaining material gain depends on rational demands for maximum utility, it is conditioned by the structure of trust, a vital factor in any organized group action. Trust springs more from values traditionally covered by religion than from rational calculations.

The renewal of Bosnia must be based on the indivisibility of economic and cultural reconstruction. This requires a clear view of the nature of the anti-Bosnian master plan, and the elites, ideologies, and organizations defined by it, who have participated or may participate in the campaign of destruction. Establishing trust capable of crossing religious and ethno-national divides demands a clear and unambiguous definition of the crimes that have taken place, and just penalties for their perpetrators. But, simultaneously, the crimes must be distinguished from the culture that was used to provide meanings, symbols, and ideas for building their ideology. Enabling dialogue between Islam and both of the Christian churches present in Bosnia is as essential as rebuilding broken roads, establishing freedom of movement for people and goods, the return of refugees, and so on.

There exist vital elements in all forms of culture in Bosnia-Herzegovina that can be linked together so that they ensure the promotion of trust. This will not destroy genuine cultural individuality, but will enable the reconstruction of unity in diversity, as the precondition for promoting general ethical norms applicable to all, regardless of their political, religious, and ethno-national differences.

Bosnia-Herzegovina's unity is inseparable from the Balkans, Europe, and the world. All aspects of this unity, in the totality of its differences, must be seen in the context of their relationship to these inner and outer circles. If the principle of linking the European nations into a harmonious community, as a precursor for closer world relationships, is betrayed in Bosnia itself—by permitting Bosnia's neighbors to succeed in their genocidal campaign—this would set a poor precedent for the future. European countries may come to fear that they will find themselves abandoned to division in the same way that Bosnia was abandoned. Therefore it is of vital importance to understand the relationship of Bosnia-Herzegovina and its distinct members to the wider currents of European policy. The Europe of the last five centuries has been the arena of many savage wars, and the risk of more is still present and immediate. The presence of American interests and power in building a European supranational political structure will play, for the next few decades, a decisive role in developing and firming the economic, cultural, and political mosaic of this continent. This trend is clearly present in the ongoing expansion of NATO toward the East. The trend will certainly continue and will act as the main impulse shaping events in Eastern European countries.

Within such an association, national states can develop their identity on the basis of unified standards of human rights, the development of ethno-national identity and security, economic growth, and the like. The borders of national states will become all the more conditioned by trends toward interassociation, and the dream of the nation state, which was the foundation of the Greater Croatian and Greater Serbian plans, will become less appealing. This movement, in the widest European terms, provides support for the establishment of Bosnia-Herzegovina as a unified state with heterogeneous relationships with its neighboring states and wider European political and cultural trends. The political and military presence of Serbia and Croatia, the main cause of the genocide and destruction in Bosnia, will lose its purpose as Bosnia and these states are drawn into the currents linking Europe, and linking Europe to the world.

This is an attempt to demonstrate the need for trust in the currents of history through which Bosnia-Herzegovina is about to pass. The ethno-national elites will try to strengthen the readings of history that justify their destructive plan. Central to their readings is the concealment and redefinition of the crimes committed in Bosnia-Herzegovina. A precedent has already been set by the treatment, in official histories, of crimes committed earlier in this region. The lack of adequate research into, and judgment of, these earlier crimes promises that the latter-day crimes will also be consigned to moral limbo and are thus unlikely to be the last of their kind. Disregard of the true definition of the crime, and failure to identify and punish the criminals, will enable the criminals to continue as before, in a fog of concessions, dirty deals, excuses, and moral ambiguity. This leads to a wider model for interpreting the war, and one already popularized. It teaches that in Bosnia there are no just people or causes: all are guilty, and only the relative quantities of guilt remain to be determined. This interpretation of Bosnia-Herzegovina's recent history threatens the remaining links of idealism and trust, without which the promise of a better future is an empty one.

18

RENEWAL AND SUSTAINABLE GROWTH

The technological development of Bosnia-Herzegovina took place mainly in the period after the Second World War, when the society of this country was a constituent part of a wider, ideologically based and managed economic and political system. The gross national product of Bosnia-Herzegovina in 1991 was U.S.$10.6 billion. This was produced by an economically active workforce of 1,300,000 people, of whom 308,000 were unemployed, with the surplus workforce numbering around 200,000. Of the total workforce, 7 percent held university diplomas, high school diplomas were held by 6 percent, and secondary school diplomas were held by around 19 percent. Seven percent of workers were highly qualified, and 30 percent were qualified. The contribution of industry and mining to the gross national product was 43 percent, agriculture and fisheries around 10 percent, engineering 8 percent, transport and communications 8 percent, trade 17 percent, and the remainder (tourism, crafts and the like) 11 percent. In the industry and mining sector of Bosnia-Herzegovina, the first place was held by the production of electricity: 9 percent of GNP came from this particular branch of the economy. Second place was held by the metal industry (8.5 percent), next came transport engineering (7.5 percent), the production of coal (7 percent), the textile industry (6.5 percent), and the leather and clothing industry (6 percent).

The economy of Bosnia and Herzegovina before the war, with its human, industrial, energy production, and agricultural potential, was semideveloped, but with good prospects for further growth. The war interrupted the barely commenced transition to a market economy and caused huge material and human damage to the economy. The estimated cost of the damage to the economy of Bosnia-Herzegovina from 1992 to 1996 is placed at around U.S.$115 billion. The GNP of 1996 was not even a quarter of what it had been in 1991. Industrial production was 90 percent down from 1991, and employment was down by 65 percent. Around 60 percent of the inhabitants lived in conditions below the poverty line, in need of help and protection.

Bosnia-Herzegovina has been left behind in terms of technological development in relation to other European countries. The war broke off connections with the outside world and caused widespread destruction. The development gap widened significantly. Education and training suffered catastrophic interruption, and closing this gap will prove difficult. The choice of technologies appropriate for Bosnia-Herzegovina is an urgent task. A united research campaign is necessary, but full awareness of this need, and the intention to address it, are lacking. The acceptance of new technologies depends on the predictability of the political, economic, and cultural development of Bosnian-Herzegovinan society. In the context of reconstructing this society, it is essential that sustainable forms of growth are promoted in tandem with the development of new technology.

Technology, as a combination of knowledge, organization, engineering, equipment, and human skill, serves both to develop and produce socially desirable and appropriate goods. The currently backward state of Bosnian-Herzegovinan society requires that the role of technology be considered in the context of overcoming political, economic, and cultural obstacles to transforming and harmonizing the main elements in its society. But this will not be possible except by evolving a new, united approach toward renewal and by strengthening social trust. The promotion of knowledge and technology through culture is needed. This should take into account the requirements and skills of all individuals and groups in Bosnia-Herzegovina. Only through systematic research will it be possible to identify a suitable policy for techno-economic development and to build the institutions and organizations that will create a suitable technological environment. We need to research all views connected with culture that will have an impact on technical change.

The plan for the economic reconstruction of Bosnia-Herzegovina that the World Bank is coordinating envisages financial support of U.S.$5.3 billion, over a period of three to four years. Of this sum, from 1996 to 1997 less than $1.5 billion was used. The plan is being implemented slowly and with many difficulties, above all internal. These obstacles include the inefficiency of institutions, the nonimplementation of the Dayton Agreement, poor personnel capacity, and the like. This plan is conditional on the transition of the economy of Bosnia-Herzegovina toward a market economy, based on privatization, medium- and small-sized industries, and appropriate state structures, which will be legally regulated, with frequent public auditing of accounts. The legal foundations of the process of economic transition are still in their infancy, and other vital preconditions for a market economy are absent. There is insufficient research into, and even public opposition to, fresh concepts of developing the economy.

The process of privatization will probably have two pillars. The first is the transition of ownership from the state to the private sector. Investors will only be interested in industries whose ownership is clear and where all owners have the common goal of making the industry profitable. The second pillar is opening access to foreign investors, who will bring with them the necessary capital. Privatization has not moved forward even now, two years after the war has stopped. Even a law to establish initial balance sheets has not yet been passed, and without it privatization cannot begin. This increases the risk of illegal privatization, with long-term political, economic, and cultural consequences. These are only some of the dangers that have the potential to spark off further phases of destruction, leading to the total collapse of the foundations of Bosnian-Herzegovinan society.

The Communist system, with all its political, economic, and cultural consequences, continued unabated in the cruelty of war. Some of its elements collapsed, but others grew stronger.

The conditions of the aftermath of war can be summarized as the destruction of the state system, alongside the establishment of new centers of power, which are clearly opposed to democratic transformation. The need for the transition of Bosnia-Herzegovina is different from that of other Eastern European borderlands of the Communist world. No consent on the underlying premises of transition has even been reached. In addition to the baggage inherited from the Communist system, the consequences of war stand in the way. There is obvious disagreement both as to the purpose and as to the methodology of transition. For example, privatization is taking place outside any transitional procedures framework, although the transition experience of other East European countries teaches that isolating the privatization process is both undesirable and impossible. This points to the need for a basic understanding and linking of privatization with other social changes.

On the other hand, the society of Bosnia-Herzegovina is extremely weak. It lacks the means and infrastructure necessary for carrying out an effective process of transition. In addition to the division caused by its internal borders, there is no structure or means for the macroeconomic management of its industry as a whole. What exists is an attenuated (and in many places undefined) political structure, combined with a lack of any unified economic arena, a lack of agreed-upon economic laws and regulations, and an absence of many other factors essential for economic growth. In such circumstances, the creation of a committed social group capable of striving to reach this target is impossible. The current shapes of political thought, and their expression in a series of social blunders, prevents any trust from being placed in the state government, so there can be no meaningful discussion on forming a systematic approach to economic development. Only if these problems are addressed will the current problems of Bosnia-Herzegovina be resolved: the survival of this state is at present only possible with a hefty foreign military presence, the investment of foreign resources, and political protection in the form of direct management of the most important political tasks. If Bosnia is to become a sustainable state, with a united internal base, an objective basis needs to be found for solving the country's problems, with a long-term plan for political, economic, and cultural change.

Thus the reconstruction of Bosnia-Herzegovina, the development of a civil society, the renewal of trust, and the affirmation of democracy are all impossible without sustainable economic growth. But this needs research aimed specifically at the economic goals of transition, in order to transform the war-devastated economy and bring in foreign investment. Research projects directed at key areas should be prioritized: establishing and developing small- and medium-sized industries, privatization, economic union, new models of employment, regional economic cooperation, and eventual economic integration in the European Community.

Bosnian culture, throughout its history, has been pluralist. The ideological picture of recent years largely ignores the elements traditional to this particular culture. This pluralism included the formal recognition, embodied in legislation, of religious freedom, in accordance with the supra-rational aspects of religious tradition. The revolutionary changes resulting from the Renaissance, the Reformation, and the Industrial Revolution, all grounded in scientific development, did not succeed in touching this aspect of Bosnian society in the sense of promoting debate about itself and its future. The ethno-national ideologies, which took the form of opposing nationalisms, were resisted by this pluralism. Only after the catastrophic impact of these ethno-national elites, ideologies, and armed organizations has any need to redefine the concept of Bosnia's unity emerged.

The recent concept of dividing the sacred from the secular elements of a culture, which found its most comprehensive expression in Communist ideology, has had its share in increasing confusion about the part played by meanings, symbols, and concepts in forming identity. This confusion has mainly showed itself in a lessening of respect for and responsibility toward the right of personal choice. The use of only one set of meanings, symbols, and concepts for the construction of identity has produced a corresponding tendency to deny or denigrate all others. Pointing out the essential equality of all different elements of culture, which is essential for coexistence in a pluralist society, is a particularly vital priority where Bosnian society is concerned. Careful construction of an agreed upon methodology for researching this and other questions is needed if answers are to be found.

Since the construction of individuality all too often starts with total denial of others, even, or especially, of those who are culturally, geographically, and historically similar, it is essential for Bosnia-Herzegovina to establish a unified approach to researching history and culture. This must be managed in a way that emphasizes both the similarities and the differences. The deepest cultural elements of religious traditions have, up to now, been largely left out of any systematic, objective examination. Thus it has been impossible to establish soundly-based relations between them. Simplified or narrow views of the individual elements of Bosnian culture are dangerous owing to the ease with which they can be exploited by political ideology. In order to develop an awareness of the different elements of cultural inheritance as a publicly, openly acknowledged good, systematic research and convincing presentation of the results is required.

Economic and political division can easily be explained with the help of a rational model. Overcoming it requires further use of the same model. But this method will not affect the more dangerous division and opposition between ideologized interpretations of culture. The consequences of the war against Bosnia include the strengthening and hardening of ideological separatism, which defines itself as "Bosniak," "Croatian," or "Serbian." The growth of these ideologies into entities complete with political and economic structures has been accompanied by a decline in their ability to start a dialogue among themselves. The desire to transcend the borders of conflict and division, however, has started to appear in the formation of a new Bosnian-Herzegovinan intellectual nucleus. Bosnian unity has a meaning and a future only if determined builders and organizers, fundamentally committed to unity in diversity, materialize in day to day life. But all attempts to construct this unity that fail to strive toward restoring trust between its Bosniak, Croatian, and Serbian elements are only ways of continuing the disintegration process, though with new methods and tactics.

19

The answer to the question of Bosnia's future depends to a large extent on American political will. After a long period of agony had been endured by Bosnia and her people, revealing a number of internal differences and oppositions within Europe itself, the United States of America took a leading role in stopping the war. However, by the manner of U.S. intervention, significant concessions were made to the destroyers of this state. For example, official recognition was given to a Serbian ethno-national state, while conditions were imposed that provided scope for the inclusion of parts of Federation territory in the structure of the Republic of Croatia. The elements of Bosnia-Herzegovina's statehood were reduced to the smallest possible extent. This was represented as the price that had to be paid for halting the killing and destruction.

The only possibilities of rebuilding and strengthening the state of Bosnia-Herzegovina are contained in various vague specifications. However, total disintegration, as proposed by the suggestion by the Contact Group of dividing the country into two halves, is not envisaged. The future of the Bosnian-Herzegovinan state depends on the guarantees for the return of refugees and displaced persons to their homes and their property, the security of all throughout the country, and the mutual respect of other rights. These are to be guaranteed by the institutions and organizations defined by the documents of the Dayton Agreement. The possible strengthening of the state is incorporated in specifications regarding unification of the monetary system, the economic arena, and foreign policy.

The American involvement is worth considering in terms of the interplay of two important aspects of American policy in the world. The first is the strong link between Europe's security and American military presence, in the form of the spread and growth of NATO. The second is that this particular world power considers itself the most important and most responsible advocate and protector of general human values. Critics of this policy, who argue against both of these roles, try by citing American involvement in solving the Bosnian tragedy to demonstrate that American presence in Europe, now that the East-West bloc division has ended, is unnecessary, and that widening NATO toward Russia works against building a better future for Europe. Certain political forces inside Europe have taken up these positions and are trying in their different ways to undermine American policy in Bosnia. This is evident in the frequent absence of any decisive action in opposing the latter-day policies of Tuđman and Milošević. The preservation of the Bosnian-Herzegovinan state requires that its unity in diversity be defended against the secret and open activities of the Greater Serbian and Greater Croatian ideological elites in pursuit of fuller division. But such defense and protection is a difficult and costly political undertaking. It can easily be challenged from the standpoint of political realism. However, the defense and preservation of the principal elements of Bosnian unity is of great importance for the future of the world, and it is worth giving careful consideration to this policy.[1] The critics of U.S. policy who are located inside the United States are aligned with the forces that stimulate and support Croatian and Serbian ethno-national goals, which demand the destruction of Bosnia as a means to their ends. This alignment is one way of opposing the American role in the world.

Taking a long-term view of possible changes in the geopolitical space of Europe is a precondition for understanding which trend—the confirmation or the destruction of Bosnia-Herzegovina's unity—will triumph. Europe is undergoing a process of wholesale geopolitical restructuring. This cannot be isolated from the course of European history, nor from current world events. After the Second World War the unification of Europe was linked with political, eco-

---

1. For the recommendations of division instead of the currently expressed desires to preserve the country's unity, see, for example, M. O'Hanlon, "Bosnia: Better Left Partitioned," *Washington Post,* 10 April 1997, A25; K. B. Hutchinson, "The Bosnia Puzzle Needs a New Solution," *New York Times,* 11 September 1997, A35; H. A. Kissinger, "Limits to What the U.S. Can Do in Bosnia," *Washington Post,* 22 September 1997, A19; and J. J. Mearschimer, "The Only Exit from Bosnia," *New York Times,* 7 October 1997, A31.

nomic, and monetary changes. Today the pattern has been reversed, with priority given to monetary union, and the acceleration of economic and political change as its result. Current trends are working toward the inclusion of those countries that have been divided from the European mainstream since 1945. Europe as a concept is widening toward the East.

But this raises the question: Where does Europe end? No clear borders exist. What is more, the further the advance is made toward the East, the vaguer the borders are. And wherever they are redrawn, a whole series of questions springs up. The movement from the Atlantic toward the East shows the complexity of European cultural and political diversity. This raises yet another question: who is closer to Europe, the Muslims on the other side of the Mediterranean, or the Christians of the Urals and the Caucasus? This question underlies any serious geostrategic consideration of the concept of Euro-Asia as a key issue in the world's future. It contains numerous unknown unities and differences, understandings and incomprehensions. Whatever the answer is, a serious reshaping of attitudes toward the political, economic, and cultural elements with which Europe is inevitably connected will be needed in the future. The process of expansion toward the East begs the question of how Europe and Russia's futures will relate to each other. Russia's entry into the European monetary, economic, and political mainstream will not be possible for a long while. But no vision of the future of Europe can exclude Russia. To become a part of Europe, Russia must pass through the changes collectively known as "transition." But this enormous country is still a long way away from completing the process and is therefore not yet ready for any significant form of union with the rest of the continent. The problems include Russia's perception of itself, since it does not regard itself as a nation-state in the European sense. The modernization process demands that the Russian imperialist consciousness become a form of national consciousness. But is this change likely?

The form Europe's future will take depends to a large extent on the answer to this question, while the American presence in Europe is connected with the uncertainty as to the answer. The greater the uncertainty, the more necessary the American presence is perceived to be.

The most significant movement in European terms is, accordingly, the gradual inclusion of the countries of Eastern Europe in the trend toward geostrategic unification. Drastic changes have taken place along the Tallinn-Warsaw-Budapest-Osijek-Mostar-Ploče axis. The geopolitical re-structuring of Europe is connected with the direct or indirect expansion of NATO eastward along this line. All events happening around it, or centered on it, reflect the most important issue for the future of Europe and the geopolitical future of the world. NATO has only extended its presence a small distance, but some regions are approaching of their own accord. Bosnia-Herzegovina's geopolitical axis lies directly along this line. The presence of NATO in Bosnia today means that this is the only region where the structure of this military organization directly borders on a range of Orthodox Eastern European countries, from Greece northward. But the most disregarded sector of this line runs through the countries of Southeastern Europe, above all those in the Eastern vicinity of Bosnia-Herzegovina (Montenegro, Serbia, Albania, and Macedonia). Addressing this deficiency, and tackling any "hot spots" of possible conflict, must include resolving the problems of Bosnia-Herzegovina.

Southeastern Europe is actively influencing the future of this continent. The establishment of Serbia and Croatia as ethno-national states, and their efforts to expand across the territory of Bosnia-Herzegovina, may further upset the geopolitical imbalance of this region. But Europe's military acceptance of an American protectorate will inevitably undergo a number of changes, depending on the development of European unification and its expansion toward the East. The more powerful and more permanent these changes are, the more clearly it will be perceived that the Bosnian-Herzegovinan model, one totally opposed to the ethno-nationalist idea, is thoroughly undesirable to any imperialist consciousness. But Europe's future depends on stopping and reshaping all imperialist policies in the association of states that form the geopolitical organization of Europe. The Transatlantic European-American alliance is, therefore, the foundation stone of future events in Europe.

The future of the world as favored by some current American —and other— ideologies includes the expansion of Western liberalism, liberal democracy, and the market economy. At the top of this structure, as model and protector, belongs the United States. The widening of U.S. influence is part of this vision of the world's future. Those who are not fully convinced by this plan cite dangers from other quarters. Those who question America's leadership do not, however, question the powers seen as hostile to the values of liberal democracy and the free-market economy—for example, the Peoples Republic of China or the Islamic Republic of Iran. New alliances, however, could develop—for example, a union between Germany, Russia, China, Iran, and Japan—that could endanger the American position in the world.

All these possibilities should be taken into consideration when analyzing NATO's movements and policies in the westernmost countries of the erstwhile Warsaw Pact. This expansion sets up a barrier to new alliances that could endanger the current world order. Germany and Japan must, for the sake of this order's future, stay "tame"—for their development into the headquarters of new political alliances would rapidly bring about a redistribution of world power. This would present a huge challenge to American hegemony in the establishment of "universal" values and liberal democracy.

American persistence in protecting and developing Bosnia's "unity in diversity" model, with its parallels to the American dream, will produce results only if a long-term and expensive presence is maintained. Every hesitation will be exploited by those forces that oppose America's role in the world and NATO's expansion toward the East. These forces will, through public promises, alliances, and other methods, increase their support for those who argue the impossibility of Bosnia and the consequent imperative of dividing the former state between Croatia and Serbia.

If the American model is to be realized by the patient accumulation of limited successes—as Henry Kissinger himself points out—a long-term American presence in Europe is necessary to enable the U.S. vision of a world of coexistent differences. Thus, the presence of NATO in Bosnia-Herzegovina can be understood as a part of that policy. Those who deny the Bosnian model and who advocate division will interpret this presence differently. They will see the Bosnia-Herzegovina segment of the Tallinn-Ploče line as a gap that must be bridged to enable the creation of two new states, one for all Serbs and one for all Croats. The ruling elites who support this interpretation will try to appear cooperative. They will cite the Bosnian-Herzegovinan state, and above all its Bosniak/Muslim element, as the main obstacle to building a Balkan bridge for widening NATO toward the East. Yet it should be remembered that it was part of the plan of these two ethno-national ideologies to create a Bosniak "third party" that could be represented as hostile to Western culture.

The full ethno-national division these elites aim for will leave no place for a third party. This threat to Bosnia must be overcome, not least because it directly counters the model of community that the United States advocates and promotes in world terms. The American presence in Bosnia should be nothing more than the protection of the bare right to survival. If it is motivated solely by compassion toward the endangered, and justice is sacrificed to political realism and motives of economy, then this will merely be one more betrayal of the model. The defense and reconstruction of Bosnia-Herzegovina's society has meaning only if those statements and acts that destroy its unity in diversity are refuted and opposed. The concept that it is impossible for Bosniaks, Croats, and Serbs to live together in one community is totally opposed to the American model and is refuted by the inner essence of Bosnian history and culture. The defense of Bosnia is not the defense of something Bosnia never was, but is, on the contrary, part of the general effort to build a sustainable world future. Unless it learns from the trust that Bosnia has succeeded in maintaining for most of its history, the future of the world is unthinkable.

But if today's European allies of the United States again become as hostile toward each other as they have been at several points during this century, post-Dayton Bosnia-Herzegovina will be in serious danger, since the Dayton Agreement presupposes cooperation between Europe and the United States. Unless strong foundations are established for Bosnia-Herzegovina now, both Europe and the United States might be forced to accept that they have remained in the prison of history instead of putting its lessons into action.

If the war against Bosnia-Herzegovina is reduced to a "conflict of civilizations," as the prime movers in this war, aided by key international political thinkers, have tried to suggest, then the criminals will be rewarded and a precedent set for the repetition of the entire cycle, in Bosnia and elsewhere. Both aims of American policy will be brought into question, and their supporters humiliated. The price of a long-term foreign presence in Bosnia-Herzegovina is not only a rhetorical question: failure to establish a sustainable social order and proper relations between all members of the Bosnian-Herzegovinan state would cost indisputably more, both in money and in lives. Without an American presence, Bosnia-Herzegovina will again present an unpalatable proof that a safe Europe is only a dream and that the reality is a multitude of unresolved dangers, with the potential for a new holocaust to be born at any moment.

In analyses of the Bosnian-Herzegovinan tragedy, support for the "divide and quit" theory still lingers, on the grounds that "unite and quit" would require a lasting military presence and a massive financial outlay. Yet this policy, if applied, would be essentially anti-European: there can be no future for a united Europe on the basis of such a model.

Unification is the precondition for lasting peace. A divided Bosnia can avoid the recurrence of genocide only with an external military presence and at huge financial cost.[2]

2. The term "holocaust" is used in this essay in its generally accepted meaning of the Nazi destruction of the Jews during the first half of this century. During 1992 and 1993 the Bosniaks frequently used it to describe what was taking place in Bosnia. As they underwent what was then a terrifyingly immediate experience, they saw, mentally and emotionally, that the same principles underlay both events. By common consensus, the Holocaust describes the plan for the total destruction of the Jews, using all the means then available to the Nazi machine. The Greater Serbian program aimed at the total destruction, by genocide if necessary, of the Muslim presence within the territory it defined as Serbian. The destruction of the Muslims was implemented in full wherever it was feasible to carry out the killings, expulsions, and erasure of every trace of Muslim presence. The comprehensiveness of the genocide was restricted only by the physical and organizational limitations of its implementers—not by the wishes of those in charge. Hence, a comparison between these two events, while of course bearing in mind their differences in magnitude, is intended to stress their similarity in principle.

It was clear from the beginning that unification, accompanied by the suppression of expansionist activities on the part of neighboring states, is the only valid answer to enable this country to become a self-sustaining part of European unity.

The guardians of Bosnia must necessarily associate themselves with those forces that are acting for the sake of the goals most often named in the concept of European unity. These guardians are threatened today by the tyranny of ethno-nationalist elites. This is demonstrated, inter alia, by the conspicuous absence of reliable and organized participants in a general plan to protect and develop Bosnia-Herzegovina in accordance with a model of Europe's likely future.

Bosnia is a name for a model of community life shared by the inheritors of different holy traditions. Its history bears witness to efforts to formalize this model in contemporary modes of thought. In an earlier period—the time of the Bosnian Bans and Kings—this model expressed itself in the effort to justify and establish communal life between different Christian communities. Interpretations of Christ developed differently in the various Christian communities. The disagreements were sometimes large, sometimes hardly noticeable. They took the forms defined as Orthodoxy, Catholicism, and the Bosnian Church. No agreements were formally established to assert that no single creed can have priority, nor that the right road lay in dialogue based on the acceptance of the faiths of all participants. But it cannot be disputed that the tolerance these communities showed each other testifies to a respect for the statement that "God gave every people their law and their way of life." The realization that other teachings might form a meaningful part of this dialogue may have been the reason for a significant number of Bosnian Church leaders to adopt Islam. This suggests that unbiased research into Bosnian history may produce the conditions necessary to reconstruct such a dialogue.

Only then will it be possible to arrive at a full definition of Bosnia's unity in diversity. In the strength of each community, based on their own holy teaching, the trust necessary for dialogue was planted. As one of God's messages runs: "Had God not driven back the people, some by the means of others, there had been destroyed cloisters and churches, oratories and mosques, wherein God's name is much mentioned." This model of mutual defence and respect has never been incorporated into a political plan, which could serve as a foundation for building a state powerful enough to defend and develop this multiplicity. But this model is present—in the form of the direct assaults committed against it— in all the policies that have been opposed to the concept of Bosnia. These proclaim the goal of "homogenization" on the basis of only one holy tradition and an ideological policy deriving from it. Thus Bosnia becomes a country where Serbian rule and Orthodoxy, or Croatian rule and Catholicism, should dominate, to the exclusion of all others: the possibility of mixed communal life, the tradition most strikingly obvious to all who view Bosnia from outside, is rigidly excluded.

This all contributes to the present reduction of Bosnia's unity in diversity to an Islamicized "Muslim" or "Bosniak" policy. This is calculated to reawaken

European images of Muslims as "Others." When the theory that agreement between the parties is fundamentally impossible has taken hold, it follows that
Bosnia-Herzegovina must be divided, if only to reduce the participation of
Muslims in the destiny of Europe. Recent efforts to interpret world events via
the "conflict of civilizations" formula are meanwhile justified with the aid of
the Bosnian example. In the resulting ideological confusion, the existence of
immutable universal laws, and the fact of their violation, is forgotten.

Bosnia is possibly the only European state where ancient ideas about the multiplicity of holy teaching have managed to obtain a foothold before being con-
sumed by the desire for nation-states. Therefore it suits both sides, Serbian and
Croatian, that Bosnia should appear to be a question soluble along strictly nationalist lines but for the obstruction of the Muslim factor. This factor had to be
presented as hostile to, and incompatible with, European culture and politics:
the campaign was immeasurably furthered by naïve nationalist ideologies produced by the Muslims themselves. Thus the three hostile forces include, in
addition to the Serbian and Croatian plans, Muslim acquiescence in, or acceptance of, the betrayal of the Bosnian model.

The international community, with all its internal oppositions, hopes to
achieve a "new world order," and this is supported today by prevailing political
orthodoxy. The plan also foresees resistance in a significant proportion of the
world. Therefore the widening of Western influence is needed to preserve
"global stability." All wars must, in accordance with this approach, be contained, so that the hostile energies inside this confined space are expended in a
way that does not endanger wider goals. The areas likely to present opposition
are, on the basis of the evidence cited by Samuel Huntington, primarily the
Confucian and Islamic worlds. Since political powers may arise in these worlds
that could oppose the West's dominance as the summit of historical development, these areas must be proved to threaten international stability. Next in line
is the peril of an alliance between the Orthodox countries and peoples. But such
an alliance is reconcilable with the cultural bases of the West, and can gradually
be incorporated in the expansion of Western presence toward the East.

A perfect model for the operation of these relationships is offered by Bosnia. Here the "Western world" has no clear borders with the "Orthodox world,"
and the situation is further complicated by the Muslim presence. The desire to
immediately fix clear borders between them is demonstrated by the position of
the Contact Group and their proposal to divide Bosnia into 49 percent and 51
percent portions—the basis of the Dayton Agreement.

Meanwhile, the representatives of the two chief ethno-national ideologies proposed that the "Serbian-Croatian conflict" could and should be solved by dividing Bosnia-Herzegovina. To bring this about the political presence of the Bosniaks had to be erased, and the method used was a campaign of genocide, implemented in all areas of Bosnia-Herzegovina where the two parties had sufficient means and strength.

The success of the anti-Bosnian ethno-national policies depends directly on the weakness of the Bosnian resistance. This weakness was ensured by reducing Bosnian policy to "Muslim" policy. Therefore the direct associates of the Serbian and Croatian destroyers of Bosnia are those advocates of a "Muslim" policy who accept that it is possible to divide Bosnia into ethno-national territories and to form ethno-national states. Both external anti-Bosnian plans depended on the growth of "Muslim policies" convinced that "everyone must have their own state."

The war against Bosnia-Herzegovina started with its declaration of independence. There was considerable division over the question of how to protect the rights arising from international acknowledgment of independence. There are two ways to interpret this division. The first sums up the case against the West, and the second argues for the defense.

The case against the West defines three aspects of the relations of the Western powers toward Bosnia. The first concerns those areas of policy and influence that are tied to "Western European civilization." This defined the West's reaction to Croatian nationalist policy. The second concerns the areas of policy and influence of the Orthodox world, which related to the contents of Serbian national policy. Since the West was persistently and energetically striving to establish contacts of cooperation and reconciliation with the Orthodox world, the West's approach to Serbian policy in Bosnia was not allowed to endanger these relations. Third, any Islamic presence, defined as a significant obstacle to the globalization of liberal democracy and the free market, was seen as a possible obstacle to the "tide of history," and hence to be suppressed.

The defense of the role of the West consists of its intermittent efforts on behalf of Bosnian statehood once the latter was acknowledged: the imposing of sanctions on Serbia, pressures on Croatia, military backing of the peace talks, the implementation of democratic elections, projects for the return of refugees, investment in reconstruction and economic growth, and much more.

The war against Bosnia and Herzegovina began at a time when political awareness of the unity of the country and its history was very weak. In the long period of growth of Serbian and Croatian ethno-national plans it became clear that the weakening of Bosnia-Herzegovina's unity was the precondition for establishing a united Serbian and a united Croatian state. The conflict between Serbs and Croats was soluble, according to these plans, "by the division of Bosnia-Herzegovina between Serbs and Croats." But the agreement was opposed by the Bosniaks. Therefore the "solution of the Bosniak-Muslim question" became central to both these plans. This was accompanied by energetic activity to establish the Croatian and Serbian states in their new borders. Bosnia-Herzegovina underwent the division of territory on the basis of "ethno-national criteria." Every community in Bosnia-Herzegovina felt compelled to define their territory and to establish ethno-national sovereignty within it.

The war was directed from the ethno-national power centers. The ideology of division was deepened by the use of force. Wherever possible, all signs of the presence of Others were excluded and destroyed. Simultaneously, "peace plans" were proposed. Every one of them—starting from the Carrington-Cutileiro plans—offered the "territorial re-definition" of Bosnia-Herzegovina into sectors where one of the three ethno-national communities would dominate—"ethno-national territories," in other words.

All peace plans—the Vance Owen Peace Plan, the Action Plan of the European Community, the Invincible Package, the Contact Group Plan, and the Dayton Agreement—supported the desires of the initiators of war. In the peace talks, some of the key participants found themselves encouraged to use all available means, including genocide, to establish a homogeneous ethno-national territory.

Bosnia-Herzegovina's population was thus reduced to "three conflicting sides." The war against Bosnia-Herzegovina appeared as a threefold matrix—Bosniaks, Serbs, and Croats. They were all associated with goals equal in principle, that is, ethno-national division. All saw unity as an illusion. The final solution was, accordingly, the adoption of Realpolitik attitudes toward those holding power and humanitarian protection for the weakest in the conflict.

All struggles to form a model for the defense and sustainability of Bosnia-Herzegovina have been ineffectual to date. Since such a model is feared by those opposed to Bosnian unity, all advocates of defense have been driven from the political arena and smeared in the eyes of the Bosnian public. All supporters of those joint patriotic associations, which in their commitment to defending Bosnia testified to its possibility as a unified state, were rejected as utopianists. In a similar manner, the possibility of constructing a systematic approach at an international level, which could seek support for the Bosnian state in the principles of the international order, was banished. The frame of defense was narrowed, and the forces of division encouraged.

The Dayton Agreement was the confirmation of this trend. It stopped the war but did not exclude either the ruling elites or the organizations of the "warring parties" from the political arena. Bosnia is theoretically possible as a unified state on the basis of this agreement, but in practice and in much of the small print it is clearly divided. The war has stopped, but its causes have not been removed. Separate military (or police) structures have been established, whose relationships with each other are those of "parties to the conflict" who have declared a cease-fire.

The situation in which Bosnia finds itself today can be seen a crossroads. From it two routes are possible, the first leading to division, by which peace would be bought with the exchange of territory. The other leads to reuniting the disconnected parts into a stable whole. Considering the events in the aftermath of the Dayton Agreement, the first road is the more likely, for within Bosnia-Herzegovina its advocates are more numerous and better organized than the opposition. Further evidence is offered by the presence of the same ethno-national elites and organizations who brought about the war toward trends of ethno-national homogenization, the nonreturn of displaced persons and refugees, the dysfunctionality of the joint bodies of Bosnia-Herzegovina, the growth of statehood in the three entities, and the like.

In the second interpretation, the Dayton Agreement offers the interconnection of the divided parts of the country as the only possibility for the future. This road is permanently open, and the presence of ethno-national elites and organizations is only a passing phenomenon.

The establishment of the rule of law is not possible without removing the current obstacles toward division. Removing these will encourage mutual trends toward multi-ethnic state unity. The present forces of division cannot survive if the Dayton Agreement is really implemented. They will try desperately to alter its contents to fit their original goals—but its acceptance will render such readings impossible.

These forces cannot build any association that would be morally and politically convincing. They can survive only as long as they are sustained in a balance of opposites. They are using themselves up faster in peace than in war, and the vacuum they will leave offers the space to founding alliances and groups that would transcend the borders of ethno-national policy and ethno-national territory.

The plans for the destruction of Bosnia contend that Bosnia as a state is not possible, since the Muslims want to establish power over the Catholics and Orthodox as a means to create a Muslim state. Therefore, it suits the destroyers that there should be these intermittent desires on the part of the Muslims, and they regularly stimulate and support such desires. In the process of "Islamiciz-ing" the organizations and institutions of state, the international community saw the betrayal of Bosnia and Herzegovina, which had been internationally recognized, and proof of the claims that the attackers of the state had raised to justify the commencement of war.

In its final result, such an "Islamification" is anti-Muslim in the fullest sense. After the evidence of this process was confirmed, the most important steps in the destruction of Bosnia-Herzegovina were taken: access was blocked to the Adriatic coast, the River Sava, and so on. The advocates of the Muslim state became the enemies of Bosnia's defenders.

In the Bosnia of today there is little or no diminution of mutual distrust, and the divisions between the entities are turning them steadily into areas of ethno-national government that communicate mainly through international media-tors, smuggling connections, and secret political meetings. No organizations that could research and develop sources of trust as a precondition for the re-covery of Bosnian-Herzegovinan society have been formed.

Although the ethno-national elites seem to have achieved the major part of their original goals, they are still blocked by the Dayton Agreement. Further overt movement in the direction of division is significantly hampered, if not disabled. The situation is further complicated by the presence of several levels of international activity. Bosnia and its divided entities are a part of global pol-itics and the global economy. Only those who stay in touch with international trends can expect to actively participate in this globalization, however. Those who are prevented from doing so by distrust of their neighbors will sink all the deeper into a psychological ghetto, losing all possibility of transcending the borders in which they have enclosed themselves. Establishing connections and dialogue with their neighbors becomes psychologically all the more difficult. The result is mere utopian dreams of distant alliances and irrational policies.

Not one of the political parties now in power can initiate or develop dia-logue based on trust between all parties. Their rule is a barrier to alternative political, economic, religious, cultural, and other connections that could ulti-mately overcome segregation. In the long term, this situation particularly en-dangers the survival of the Bosniaks themselves, although their current illusory protection conceals this fact. They are left without a foundation or framework for long-term development. The Bosniaks are a people whose sur-vival is endangered. This fact is worth putting squarely before them and before all the participants in the Bosnian drama. Its concealment endangers all possi-bility of change.

The Bosnian-Herzegovinan drama can have no positive outcome if this is not founded on those elements of trust between Bosniaks, Croats, and Serbs that have been excluded by ethno-national politics. There is no future if dialogue within Bosnia is confined to the context of homogenizing policies and ethnic territories.

Bosnia needs a structured political basis on which to enter the third Christian millennium. The Dayton Agreement stopped the killing and made a start, however minute, toward reunion and the renewal of trust. However, its validation in terms of the aim of preserving and strengthening Bosnia's unity depends on at least nine points:

Freedom of movement throughout the whole of the territory, with the establishment of legal supervision of the entire state border;

The return of refugees and displaced persons to their homes and the possibility of conditions of living and employment that accord with European standards;

Dismantling of anti-Bosnian ideologies and organizations;

Trial and punishment for all those guilty of crimes against Bosnia's people;

The exclusion of all illegal activities by Serbia and Croatia in the affairs of Bosnia-Herzegovina;

The protection of economic unity by establishing customs supervision at international borders, with total freedom of movement across interentity lines;

Establishing a united plan for the economic reconstruction and development of Bosnia-Herzegovina in the framework of European ties, with the simultaneous promotion and encouragement of those forms of Bosnian culture that have the potential to revive and develop trust between the separate elements in Bosnia's unity;

The united planning and implementation of economic transition and privatization, the revival of property rights, the preventing of mismanagement and misuse of money and public assets on the basis of political power;

Limiting the capacity of the ethno-national elites to promote their anti-Bosnian ideology through public information and the education systems, the police, the army, and so on.

The intention to destroy Bosnia-Herzegovina was supported by the theory of division as the only way of balancing the opposing sides, although the subsequent tide of destruction and the conditions of the peace agreement clearly show that this approach was mistaken—and, indeed, an accessory to crime. Establishing a lasting peace requires the removal of the effects of this approach.

A lasting peace is possible only on the basis of accepting unification and state sovereignty of a kind equivalent to that of Croatia and Serbia. This is the basis on which the whole region must be evaluated.

The Dayton Agreement is a byword for success in stopping the Bosnia-Herzegovina genocide. Like every success, it is limited by what defines it. It stopped the war, but it accepted and legalized, at least partially, the goals and architects of the war. It confirmed the legitimacy of the ethno-national elites and organizations that were responsible for the war. It is a success only because the destruction was not total and because hope remains.

Nobody can call this success total as long as it does not ensure the punishment of the criminals and justice for those against whom the crimes were committed. But it was a mercy in that it stopped the killing. This success was brought about by the United States and was achieved by none of those who tried earlier, when American will was lacking. Bosnia and Herzegovina is only partially what its destroyers wanted, and its defenders are not defeated.

The political unity of the Bosnian-Herzegovinan state, as defined by the Dayton Agreement, must be established by the presidency, the parliament, the council of ministers, the constitutional court, and the central bank. But none of these can overcome the power of the three anti-Bosnian forces. All this structure, together with the supervision and action of the High Representative of the International Community, is not enough to establish a lasting peace. This still depends on the presence of international military forces.

It is necessary, therefore, to keep in view the fact that the military forces on which the current peace is founded will sooner or later be withdrawn. A new war will not bubble up in their wake only if, during their presence, a balance of military forces is created, or if sufficient trust develops between the two elements of Bosnia-Herzegovina.

Three factors are decisive for the future of Bosnia-Herzegovina:

The withdrawal of NATO;

The creation of a military balance; and

The creation of a new political force for Bosnian-Herzegovinan unity.

The withdrawal of NATO will always be a difficult issue. The public and government of the United States will never cease to consider the benefits of withdrawal.

Establishing a military balance by equipping and training the Federation Army, and above all its Bosniak component, will be represented as fulfilling a moral obligation toward an unarmed people, which was abandoned to genocide for three and a half years. But this will nevertheless be a force dividing the

Bosniak people further still from Bosnia's unity in diversity, reducing it to an ethno-national body resembling the forces that destroyed the country. The reconstruction of Bosnia-Herzegovina will seem utopian, and less and less energy will be invested in the idea.

The current Realpolitik approach is a dangerous investment for the future. The first two factors—the eventual withdrawal of troops and the militarization of the "third party"—may well work in favor of those who considered the division of Bosnia-Herzegovina as a motive for war.

Only the third factor—building trust—remains.

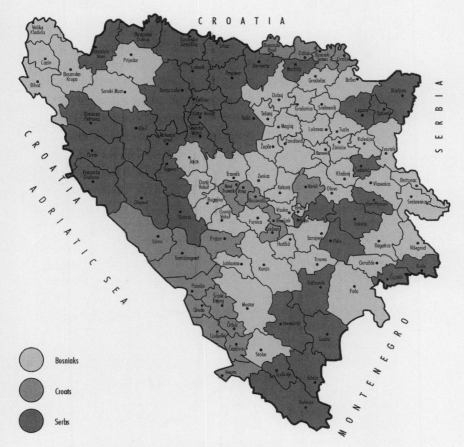

Map 1 Demographic, cultural, economic, and political unity

The demographic distribution of Bosniaks, Croats, and Serbs on Bosnia-Herzegovina's territory, shown on the basis of the 1991 census, is the result of several centuries of demographic development. The presence of Muslims, Catholics, and Orthodox (that is, Bosniaks, Croats, and Serbs) in each individual area of Bosnia-Herzegovina was mixed, a quality that was not lost through more than five centuries. This is clearly shown by the presence of religious cultural monuments of all religious communities in all areas. No internal borders ever arose so as to form distinct territorial entities for the individual ethnic participants in Bosnia's unity. Accordingly, it is not possible to say that certain Bosnian-Herzegovinan areas were ever exclusively Bosniak, Croat, or Serb on the basis of demographic evidence. The whole of Bosnia-Herzegovina's territory is, when seen in the framework of its historic and cultural elements, simultaneously Bosniak and Croat and Serb. Ideological sectarianism, however, comes into conflict with this unity and tries to lock Bosnia-Herzegovina's individual elements into different ethno-national plans.

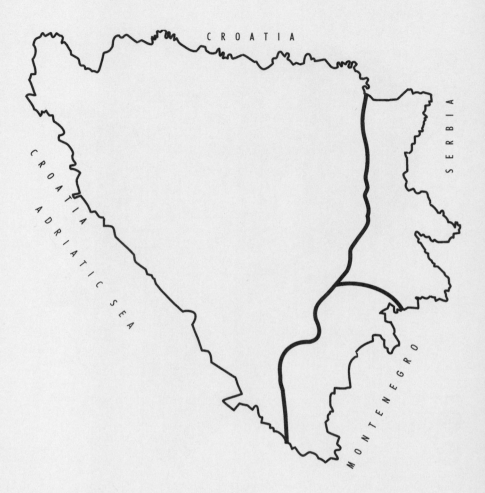

Map 2 The whole and more, the whole or a part

According to J. Cvijić, Bosnia-Herzegovina is "the central province and nucleus" of the Serb nation. Therefore the ethno-national plans for Greater Serbia cover the whole of this country and more. If this is not possible, the request is reduced to the whole or most of the whole. "The least with which Serbia can be satisfied," Cvijić wrote in 1908, "is the river boundary between the Bosna and the Drina, the Neretva and the Trebišnjica." Therefore, which demand—the greater or the smaller—is to prevail depends on the force required to remove the opposing obstacles, which include, above all, the Bosnian element. In this, Serbia's partners are those who wish to misunderstand, deny, and destroy these "obstacles." King Alexander summed up this idea in a message to Ban Milosavljević: "Be decisive, don't give in [to the Bosnian idea] and axe it at the root, while continuing a frontal attack."

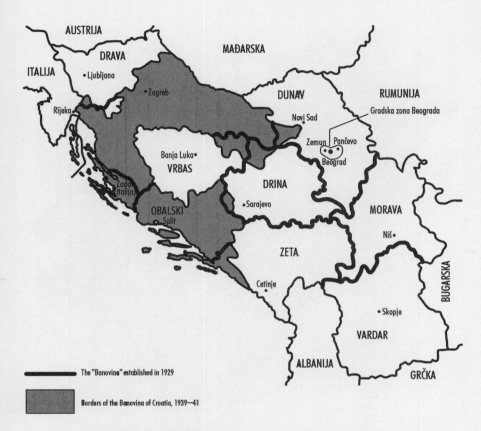

The "Banovina" established in 1929

Borders of the Banovina of Croatia, 1939—41

Map 3 The division of Bosnia-Herzegovina between the Croats and Serbs, according to the Cvetković-Maček Agreement of 1939

On the basis of the peace agreement signed on 10 September 1919 in Saint Germain, Bosnia-Herzegovina in its historic borders became part of the Kingdom of the Serbs, Croats, and Slovenes. This new state denied and weakened all elements of Bosnia's political, economic, and cultural unity. This attitude reached its peak in the division of 1939 and the establishment of Croatian Banate. This agreement, it was claimed, would "sort out" relations between Serbs and Croats. Behind such a division stood a systematic anti–Bosnia-Herzegovina ethno-national ideology working for the general good of "all Croats" and "all Serbs." These ideologies have always had their opponents among the Serbs and Croats themselves. Among people in- and outside of Bosnia there were those who thought it criminal. But the ethno-national elites tied to the ethno-national ideologies considered these antagonists as traitors, and not infrequently persecuted them. Josip Markušić complained in 1939 of the force used against his Bosnian homeland: "There is not one Croat or Serb or Slav who should allow the Country of Bosnia to be violated."

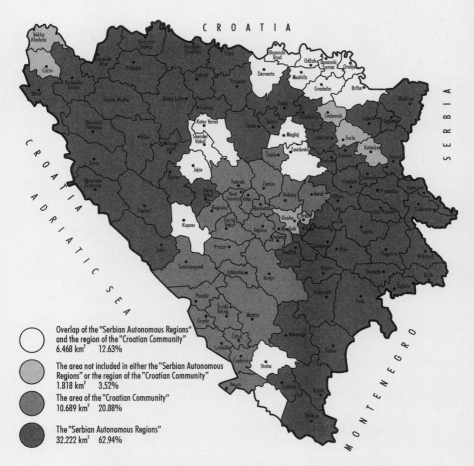

Map 4 The division of Bosnia-Herzegovina between the Serbs and the Croats

The division of Bosnia and Croatia, as demanded by the Greater Serbian and Greater Croatian ruling elites, is possible only by breaking its unity. Since that unity is of a political, economic, and cultural nature, its denial requires the promotion of ideologies that deny the heart of Bosnia-Herzegovina's being. Offering a "Muslim state" is an integral part of this destruction, since it is needed to help in tying the Bosnian Serbs and Bosnian Croats to their respective ethno-national ideologies and to delegitimize Bosnia-Herzegovina's statehood. The proposal for division "between Serbs and Croats" was raised again in 1991 and 1992 but was connected to the proposal of 1939 known as the Cvetković-Maček Agreement. These plans totally denied the facts of demographic distribution and the cultural indivisibility of Bosnia-Herzegovina as a whole.

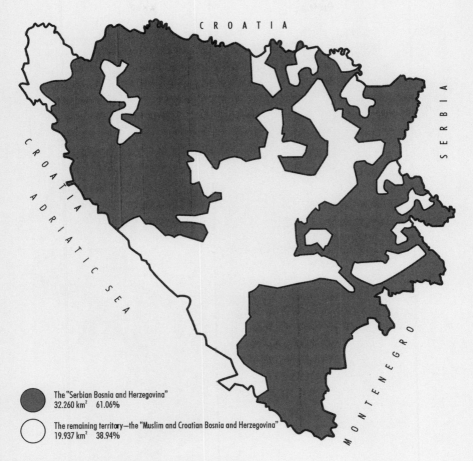

Map 5 The division proposal of March 1992

The anti-Bosnian forces offered the reduction of the country into "ethno-national territories." Since it was not possible to establish such territories on the basis of the criteria offered, the denial of Bosnia-Herzegovina's being in the framework of ethno-national ideology and its division by the use of force became the way to achieve the ethno-national goal of one state for all Serbs. In reaction to that came the propaganda and action in pursuit of the goal of one state for all Croats. For both, the destruction and division of Bosnia became the main means. The war against Bosnia-Herzegovina was arranged by the anti-Bosnian elites, ideologies, and organizations. Its principal feature was genocide. The given map is only one such example. The same element is present in all approaches, starting from the premise that individual ethno-national groups in Bosnia-Herzegovina correspond to defined ethno-national territories.

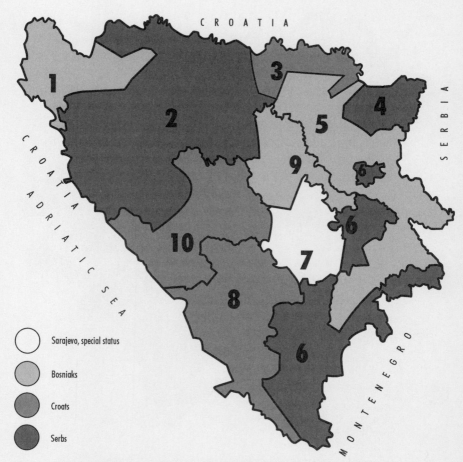

Map 6 The Vance-Owen Peace Plan: Hiding and protecting destruction

By using all available means from ex-Yugoslavia (military, secret service, finance, communications, and so on), the Greater Serbian elite unleashed the destruction of Bosnia-Herzegovina in 1991. In all territories where the resistance was insufficiently strong, the non-Serb inhabitants were expelled, killed, or arrested and all elements of culture that did not belong to the Serb faction were destroyed. Simultaneously, peace talks took place. During these talks, amid all the killing, no crime was identified but only the need for reconciling the "conflicting parties." By this Bosnia-Herzegovina's unity was forcibly reduced to mechanically divided parts, which concealed and protected the use of military force and genocide.

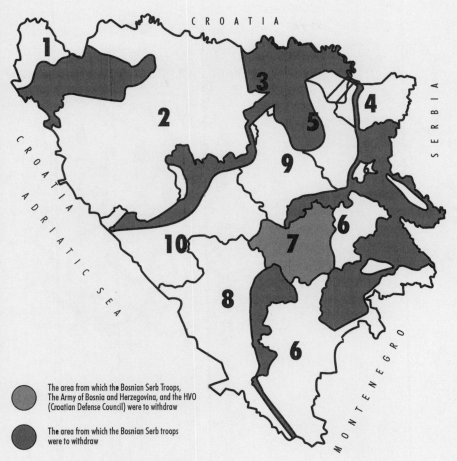

Map 7 The sham of "returned territories"

In order to carry out the reduction of Bosnia-Herzegovina's unity into "three opposing and warring parties" between which "a just peace agreement" had to be achieved, an arrangement of ethno-national territories was offered. In the first period of such a proposal (the Vance-Owen Peace Plan, 1993) the borders of "provinces" were defined. From some of them the occupying Serb army would have had to withdraw. Thus, in the middle of the drama of war the "withdrawal of the Serbian army" was proposed. Refusing this proposal meant the deepening of war, and its acceptance meant legalizing what had been gained by the use of force and genocide. This opened the doors to accepting the effects of destroying Bosnia-Herzegovina to Serb advantage.

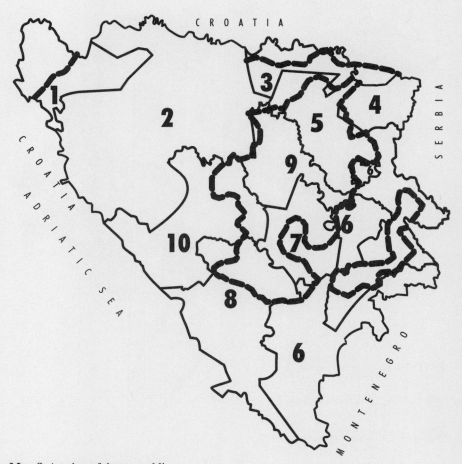

Map 8 A union of three republics

As soon as the question of ethno-national territories, which "all three opposed and warring parties" accepted, was put at the center of the peace talks, the logical consequence was the proposal of the restructuring of Bosnia-Herzegovina as a "union of three republics." This suggestion was raised by the "Serb side" in June 1993 and accepted by the "Croat side." By this, Bosnia-Herzegovina's unity was reduced to "three ethno-national entities," of which two were essentially tied to the two neighboring Greater-states, and the third stood in the way of both of them.

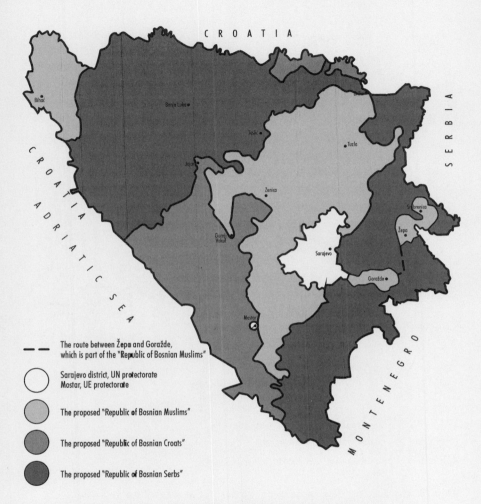

The route between Žepa and Goražde,
which is part of the "Republic of Bosnian Muslims"

Sarajevo district, UN protectorate
Mostar, UE protectorate

The proposed "Republic of Bosnian Muslims"

The proposed "Republic of Bosnian Croats"

The proposed "Republic of Bosnian Serbs"

Map 9 The union of three republics: The acceptance of destruction

When "all three opposed and warring parties" (the model underlying the plan to destroy Bosnia-Herzegovina) accepted "division," a divided international community accepted their "agreed" decision. By this they accepted the ideological position that the Bosnian-Herzegovinan ethno-national groups had always lived in mutual hatred, and that the only solution was that they should be divided into separate states. Such a view totally ignored the real nature of the plan for "dividing Bosnia between the Croats and Serbs" as "the best solution for establishing lasting peace in this part of Europe."

Map 10 The sham of "compensating the weaker side in the conflict" revisited

The suggestion of a "union of three republics" involved the acceptance of the effects of destruction and genocide. Delegitimizing the Bosnian-Herzegovinan state was reduced, according to this, into a "three-way division" by mutual agreement. The sham lies in the fact that the Bosniaks were offered territories that were under the military control of the Serbs. They would get, according to this plan, those territories for which they were already fighting with small prospect of success. Again the fundamental issue of Bosnia-Herzegovina's unity was totally obscured, and "Bosniak policy" was hoodwinked by this deception.

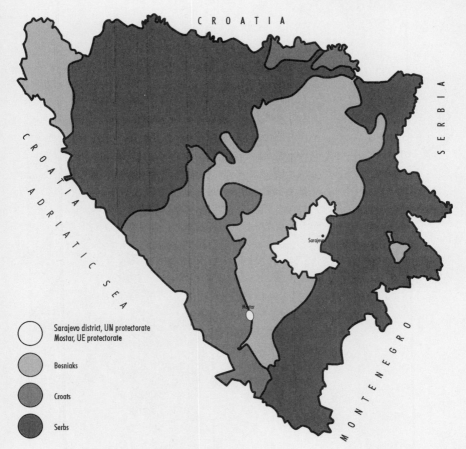

Map 11 The Owen-Stoltenberg Plan

Although this plan (August 1993) includes constitutional principles that confirm the sovereignty and independence of Bosnia and Herzegovina, it is actually "an acceptable beginning for further dialogue," as Radovan Karadžić called it. Defining the provinces in which one of the participants in Bosnia-Herzegovina's unity would, on the basis of their original war plan, gain ethno-national power represented a weakening of this unity and an acceptance of the ideology of division, the effects of war, and the unpalatable fact of "political realism." This is yet another step in reducing Bosnia-Herzegovina's unity into three totally separate elements. Such an approach includes the equalizing of guilt of all parties in Bosnia-Herzegovina, thus softening, if not completely excluding, the responsibility of the main instigators of the destruction. This involves the logical matrix of territorial division between Serbs and Croats. The plan itself is a step toward this goal and gives support to the strategy by which it is to be achieved. Zbigniew Brzezinski called the authors of this plan "negotiators whose founding concept about mixing with the parties is to negotiate endlessly, convincing the aggressors that their use of force would never be met with contrary force." He added, "the mass killings are supported, and ethnic cleansing, not to speak of mass rapes, is tolerated."

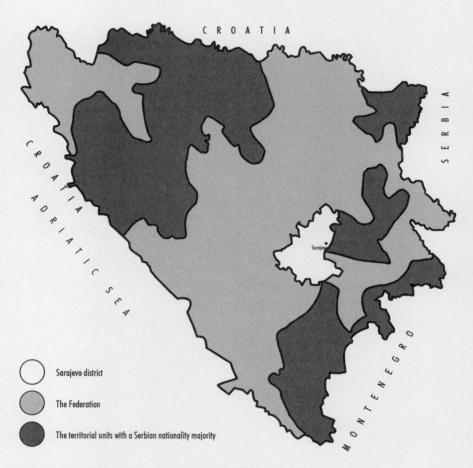

Map 12 The Federation, according to the Washington Agreement

Since not one part of Bosnia-Herzegovina could fulfill or even approach the requirement that in the divided parts a decisive majority of one people should be present, the Washington Agreement (May 1994) is, for Tuđman and the advocates of his plan of "dividing Bosnia between Croats and Serbs," a step toward his founding goal. He interpreted this agreement as placing half of Bosnia under the protectorate of the Republic of Croatia. In accordance with such an interpretation, it would follow that inside this half of Bosnian-Herzegovinan territory the systematic destruction of all remaining Bosnian-Herzegovinan political will would have to be carried out, above all by reducing it to "Muslim politics" or by accusing it of unsustainability in its present form.

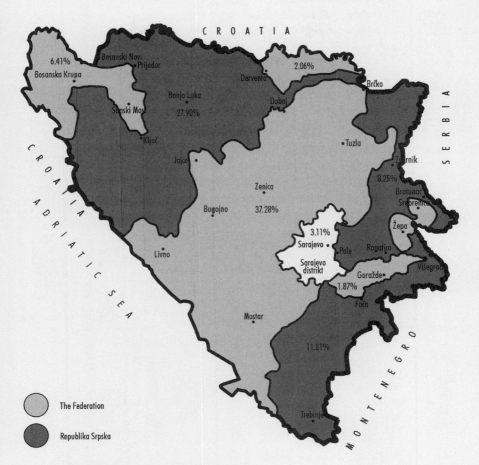

Map 13 The plan of the Contact Group

This plan incorporated the original intentions of the instigators of war against Bosnia-Herzegovina. Accepting a "Muslim" state delegitimized the policy of Bosnian-Herzegovinan unity. The goal that the Bosniaks allegedly favored before the war proved to be a deception. The claim of the destroyers, that Bosnian-Herzegovinan unity was only a propaganda trick on the part of the Muslims and that their real goal was a "Muslim state," was proved when there turned out to be a move toward accepting the proposal for a Muslim state as an answer to the original two-way division, as in the original plan of Milošević and Tuđman (see Map 4).

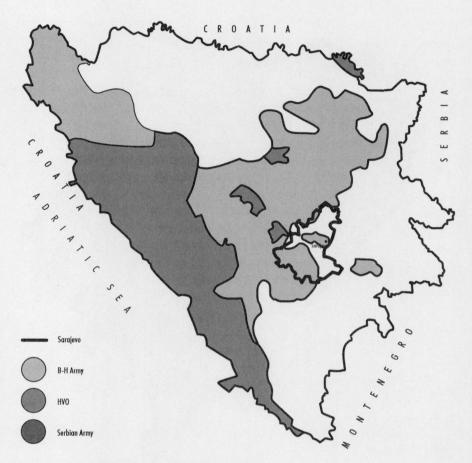

Map 14 The military situation in October 1995

The destruction of Bosnia and Herzegovina was carried out on the basis of a carefully drawn plan. This was the basis of the strategy for the division of the country between Serbs and Croats. The "necessary" restructuring was invoked as the cause of political disagreement. By long-prepared economic and military means, war was started as a way of forcing an agreement. Every approach to agreement was accepted as a "starting point for reaching final agreement." At the same time, all available means were used to destroy all elements of Bosnia-Herzegovina's unity. Participation in talks meant support and justification of all that had been achieved by war. The majority of the talks were used as preparation and justification of what was achieved by war, including genocide in the fullest sense of the word (acting with the intent that any national, ethnic, or religious group should be totally or partially destroyed).

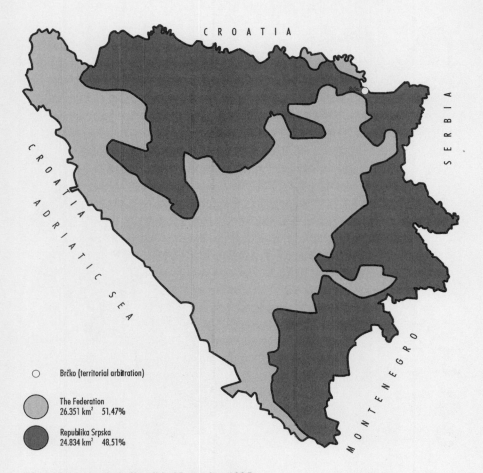

Map 15 "Interethnic lines" in November 1995

Defining the "ethnic territories" as parts of Bosnia-Herzegovina that belong only to one ethnic community requires the denial of her culture and history. The growth of any one people is only the branch of a tree that includes numerous other growths. Every Bosnian-Herzegovinan ethno-national element can be said to be rooted in the trunk of Bosnian-Herzegovinan unity, regardless of what part of her territory this community occupies at any particular time. Therefore it is axiomatic that the destruction of the country requires proof of the "division" of the elements from the whole of Bosnia-Herzegovina's culture and history. But this is possible only by reducing her historical and cultural unity into an ethno-national ideology incorporated in one ruling elite and organization.

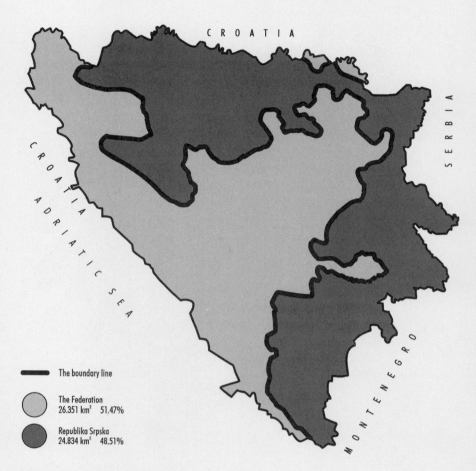

Map 16 The effects of war

Even those forces in the world that sensed the reasons and had the will to help to preserve Bosnia-Herzegovina's unity were faced with the hard-core Greater Serbian and Greater Croatian elites and organizations and their requests for division. The patriotic forces were narrowed down all the more to "Bosniak" forces, which always meant the same as "Muslim." But this was actually one of the methods of destruction. Thus the weakening of patriotic unity, and the lack of serious advocates from those centers of power in the world that could have supported such unity, formed the basis for a *realpolitik* solution. The division of Bosnia-Herzegovina "between Serbs and Croats" was accepted, and the movers of war considered that they would in peace achieve the planned division and political reduction of the Bosniaks. But the "divide and quit" theory targeted in the peace talks showed itself to be deficient. A sustainable peace required a "unite and quit" approach.

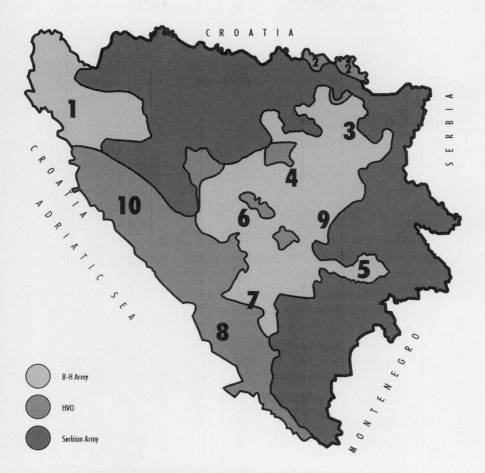

Map 17 The dissolution of demographic and political unity

War established three military-political entities: "Bosniak," "Croat," and "Serb." There is little or no freedom of movement between them. The right of the displaced to return is, years after the signing of the Dayton Accords, only an empty word, a paper promise. Demographic mutilation was the goal of those who, by the peace agreement, were accepted as the legitimate rulers of their ethno-national territories.

Population March 1992

Population March 1996

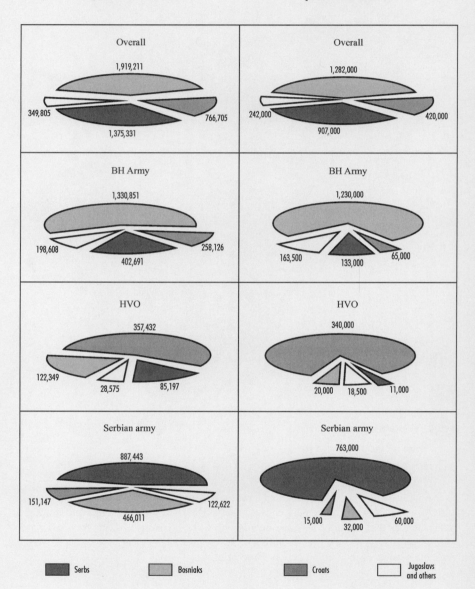

Overall
1,919,211
349,805
766,705
1,375,331

Overall
1,282,000
242,000
420,000
907,000

BH Army
1,330,851
198,608
258,126
402,691

BH Army
1,230,000
163,500
65,000
133,000

HVO
357,432
122,349
28,575
85,197

HVO
340,000
20,000
18,500
11,000

Serbian army
887,443
151,147
122,622
466,011

Serbian army
763,000
15,000
32,000
60,000

Serbs   Bosniaks   Croats   Jugoslavs and others

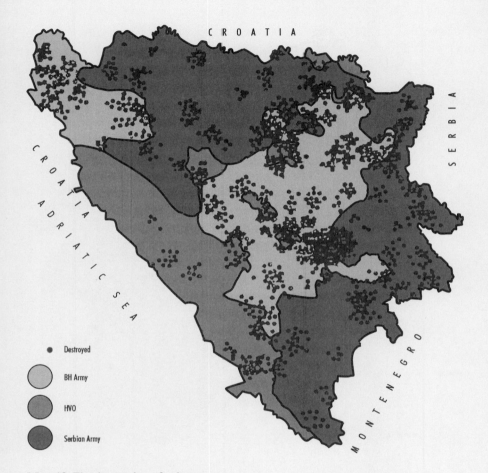

Map 18 The destruction of culture

The destruction of Bosnia-Herzegovina was carried out on the basis of a systematic plan, with history and culture at its root. Its realization required the persistent weakening of all elements of unity and the establishment of irreconcilable sectarian ideologies. The elites, ideologies, and organizations of the Greater Croatian and Greater Serbian plans were largely in agreement concerning the Muslims. They are, according to these plans, the main obstacles to division. Their weakening and destruction is the key, the elites considered, to solving the relations between Serbs and Croats. Therefore the destruction of their cultural base was crucial. This map shows the mosques destroyed in the period of 1991 to 1995 in the various military-political territories.

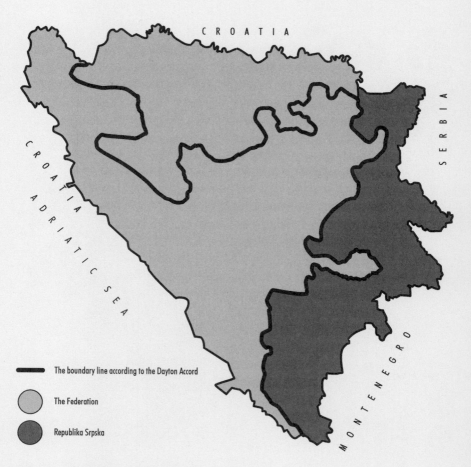

Map 19 The persistence of old plans

At the end of 1997, I. Daalder, a high official of the American analytical service, suggested the removal of obstacles to the Bosnian-Herzegovinan state on the basis of the Dayton Agreement. By this was foreseen the establishment of an independent Serb state in the eastern region, while the part west of Brcko was to be included in the Federation. The eastern part was accepted as an ethno-national Serb state, and the remaining part as a multiethnic state in which a satisfactory situation should be achieved for all Serbs and Croats throughout. This only repeats the position of J. Cvijić from 1908 as to the "minimum with which the Serbs can be satisfied." But actually this suggestion testifies to the sustainability of Bosnia-Herzegovina. If its western part must be multiethnic, just as it is in its entirety, is there any logical reason why it is unviable as a political, economic, and cultural whole?

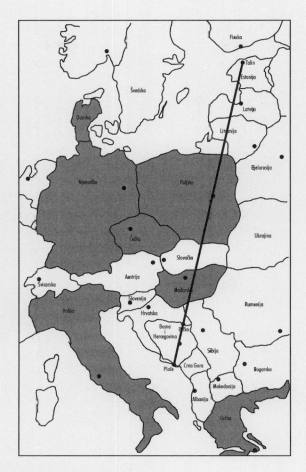

Conclusive Map The riddle of geostrategic axes

The future of Europe is defined by the method and speed of the unification of its parts west and east of the Tallinn-Ploče axis. This depends largely on the role of Russia, China, and the Central Asian links. But Bosnia is on both sides of this axis. Therefore, its existence is important in a significantly wider framework. Its people must understand their role in building the future in accordance with the inevitable trends of history. The unification of Europe requires the shaping of a consciousness of political, economic, and cultural diversity. The open-door policy toward the new members of NATO that are either on the Tallinn-Ploče axis or east of it gives all these countries a choice: to participate in or to oppose this current of history.

Rusmir Mahmutćehajić is one of Bosnia's leading public intellectuals. A dissident during the Communist years, he was elected vice president of the Bosnia-Herzegovina Government in 1991, serving under Alija Izetbegović and holding the post of Minister of Energy, Mining, and Industry. He played a critical role in attempts to gain international recognition for Bosnia-Herzegovina, but resigned from all government functions at the end of 1993 in protest against the acceptance by the greater part of the political establishment that Bosnia should be divided into ethnic parts. Since then he initiated the founding of the International Forum "Bosnia," a nongovernment organization that brings together the leading intellectuals of Bosnia and Herzegovina, in the effort to create and strengthen a civil society founded on dialogue and trust, human rights, and the rule of law.

Mahmutćehajić was born in 1948 in Stolac (Bosnia and Herzegovina). He graduated in 1973 from the University of Sarajevo and received his M.A. in 1975 and his Ph.D. in 1980 from Zagreb University. He specialized at the International Center for Theoretical Physics in Trieste, Italy, in 1982, and conducted his postdoctoral studies at the Catholic University at Louvain (Belgium). He has worked as a researcher and manager of the Institute of Safety of the Sarajevo University and as the manager of the Institute of Ergonomics at the same university. Between 1985 and 1991 he was professor and dean of the Faculty of Electrical Engineering of Osijek University (Croatia).

In addition to holding numerous academic, professional, and political posts, he was also president of the editorial board of the philosophy journal *Dialogue*. He is now co-editor of the journal *Forum Bosnae*. In his field of scientific specialization he has published more than one hundred professional and scientific works including eight books. In addition, he has published eighteen prose books, philosophical and political essays, and several translations in the Bosnian language.

Other Works by Rusmir Mahmutćehajić

Original works

Krhkost (Sarajevo, 1977)
Krv i tinta (Sarajevo, 1983)

Original works *(continued)*

Zemlja I more (Sarajevo, 1986)
Živa Bosna (Ljubljana, 1994, 1995)
Living Bosnia (London, 1996)
O nauku znaka (Sarajevo, 1996)
Dobra Bosna (Zagreb, 1997)
Kalografski listovi ćazima hadžimejića (Sarajevo, 1997)

Translations

M. Lings, šta je Sufizam? (Zagreb, 1994)
T. Burckhardt, uputa prema unutarnjem učenju Islama (Zagreb, 1994)
Ali ibn ebi Talib, nehdžu-l-belaga, with M. Hadžić (Zagreb, 1994)
M. Lings, Muhammed (Ljubljana, 1995)
Imam Ali ibn el-Husejn, sahifa, with M. Hadžić (Sarajevo, 1997)
Rene Guenon, osvriti na tesavuf i tao (Sarajevo, 1998)